I0621678

THE EXTRAORDINARY
WITHIN

The Extraordinary Within

A 7-Step Guide to Recognizing Your Potential and Achieving the Impossible

DESMOND ERIC KETTER, LPC

Scripted Mind Publishing, LLC

The Extraordinary Within: A 7-Step Guide to Recognizing Your Potential and Achieving the Impossible

© 2024 Scripted Mind Inc. All rights reserved.

First published October 14, 2024.

Republished 2026 by Scripted Mind Publishing LLC, a brand of Scripted Mind Inc.

Written by Desmond Eric Ketter, LPC.

Cover design by Abdulqoyum Abiola.

Printed in the United States of America.

No part of this publication may be reproduced, distributed, transmitted, stored in a retrieval system, or utilized in any form or by any means—electronic, mechanical, photocopying, recording, or otherwise—without prior written permission of the publisher, except for brief quotations used in critical reviews, academic work, or other uses permitted under applicable copyright law.

Scripture quotations are taken from The Holy Bible, New International Version® (NIV®). Copyright © 1973, 1978, 1984, 2011 by Biblica, Inc.® Used by permission. All rights reserved worldwide.

Publisher's Note: This publication is intended for educational and informational purposes only. It is not a substitute for professional mental health, medical, or psychological advice. Readers are encouraged to seek professional guidance where appropriate.

For permission requests, licensing, speaking engagements, or bulk purchases, contact:

Scripted Mind Publishing LLC

www.scriptedmind.co

info@scriptedmind.co

LIBRARY OF CONGRESS CATALOGING-IN-PUBLICATION DATA

Names: Ketter, Desmond Eric, author.

Title: The Extraordinary Within: A 7-Step Guide to Recognizing Your Potential and Achieving the Impossible / Desmond Eric Ketter.

Description: Tulsa, Oklahoma: Scripted Mind Publishing LLC, 2026 | Originally published: Sacramento: Legacy Lantern Publishing House, 2024 | Includes bibliographical references.

Identifiers:

ISBN 9798990557857 (print)

ISBN 9798990557871 (ebook)

Subjects: BISAC SEL027000 SELF-HELP / Personal Growth / Success.

Classification: LCC BF637.S8 K47 2024 | DDC 158.1—dc23

ISBN: 9798990557857

First Edition (2024)

This book is dedicated to my beloved wife,
Pheona
and my children, Noah, Nathan, Naomi, Nehemiah,
and Noelle Kumba.

With all a husband's and father's love.

CONTENTS

PREFACE

Welcome to "The Extraordinary Within: A 7-Step Guide to Recognizing Your Potential and Achieving the Impossible". This book is designed to help you uncover the hidden potential within yourself and guide you through actionable steps to achieve what you once thought was impossible. Each step focuses on a critical aspect of personal growth, providing you with the tools and strategies needed to transform your life.

This book isn't a quick-fix solution that promises to transform your life overnight. Instead, it is a collection of evidence-based research, practical exercises, and lived experiences that have guided me—and will guide you—in discovering your extraordinary self.

If you find the concepts in this book challenging or seemingly out of reach, I urge you to approach them with an open mind. True change requires the right tools, knowledge, and, most importantly, a willingness to try. Adopting a growth mindset will open you to new possibilities, whereas deeming something too difficult can create resistance that prevents you from even starting. Learning and applying the strategies in this book is crucial, but your motivation and commitment are essential to making meaningful progress. This isn't magic; it's about making purposeful decisions to grow.

Are you ready to discover the extraordinary potential within you?

Each step in this book is backed by research and personal experience. To discover the extraordinary within myself, I had to break free from a mindset that held me back. This meant distancing myself from naysayers and those who told me it was impossible. To achieve something extraordinary, you must be willing to do what no one else has done or is willing to do. You must defy the status quo and go against all odds. In the end, it's your efforts that count far more than any perceived shortcomings because, even if you fail, at least you tried. Failures are not defeats; they are stepping stones toward growth and success. This is what separates the doers from the spectators.

I am reminded of the powerful words by Theodore Roosevelt in his "*Man in the Arena*" speech:

"It is not the critic who counts; not the man who points out how the strong man stumbles, or where the doer of deeds could have done them better. The credit belongs to the man who is actually in the arena, whose face is marred by dust and sweat and blood; who strives valiantly; who errs, who comes short again and again, because there is no effort without error and shortcoming; but who does actually strive to do the deeds; who knows great enthusiasms, the great devotions; who spends himself in a worthy cause; who at the best knows in the end the triumph of high achievement, and who at the worst, if he fails, at least fails while daring greatly, so that his place shall never be with those cold and timid souls who neither know victory nor defeat."

Embrace this journey with courage and determination, and you will discover the extraordinary within you.

INTRODUCTION

Unlocking the Extraordinary Within

Every person has the potential to achieve greatness, to unlock the extraordinary within themselves, and to accomplish what might seem impossible. Yet, many of us go through life without fully realizing this potential, held back by limiting beliefs, negative thoughts, and a lack of clear direction. This book, *The Extraordinary Within: A 7-Step Guide to Recognizing Your Potential and Achieving the Impossible*, is a roadmap designed to help you break free from those constraints, discover your true capabilities, and embark on a transformative journey toward extraordinary success.

Who This Book Is For

This book is for anyone who feels there is more to life than what they are currently experiencing, but who may be uncertain about how to access it. Whether you are a young professional just starting out, a mid-career individual looking for a change, or someone simply seeking to improve their personal and professional life, this guide is for you. It is especially valuable for those who:

- **Feel Stuck or Unfulfilled:** If you sense that you're not living up to your potential, or you're yearning for a change but don't know where to start, this book will provide the insights and tools to help you move forward.
- **Struggle with Self-Doubt:** For those who struggle with self-confidence, who question their abilities or worth, this book will help you overcome limiting beliefs and build a strong foundation of self-belief.
- **Seek Personal Growth:** If you're committed to continuous learning and self-improvement, this book offers a structured approach to achieving ongoing growth and development.
- **Aspire to Leadership:** For those who aspire to lead—whether in their personal lives, at work, or in their communities—this book provides strategies for building resilience, embracing risk, and leading with confidence.

What's In It for You?

This book offers you more than just motivation; it provides a comprehensive guide to transforming your life. Each step is designed to build upon the last, equipping you with practical tools, actionable strategies, and a mindset shift that will enable you to achieve extraordinary success. Here's how it will help you:

- **Discover Your Potential:** You'll learn how to identify your unique strengths and talents, and how to leverage them to create opportunities and achieve your goals.
- **Overcome Barriers:** You'll gain insights into how limiting beliefs and negative thoughts can hold you back, and you'll learn techniques to overcome these barriers and build lasting confidence.
- **Craft a Vision:** You'll be guided through the process of identifying your purpose, setting SMART goals, and creating a clear vision that aligns with your aspirations.
- **Enhance Your Skills:** You'll explore essential skills like time management, prioritization, and continuous learning that are crucial for maintaining momentum and staying focused on your path to success.
- **Build Strong Networks:** You'll understand the importance of networking, mentorship, and support systems, and how to cultivate these relationships to enhance your personal and professional life.
- **Develop Resilience:** You'll discover how to build

resilience, learn from failure, and embrace risk as part of your journey toward achieving the impossible.

- **Cultivate Character:** This book contains insights to harness essential character traits that will help you grow and cement extraordinary success in your personal and professional lives.
- **Celebrate and Sustain Success:** You'll learn the importance of celebrating milestones, sustaining progress, and giving back, ensuring that your success is not only achieved but also maintained and shared with others.

How This Book Will Help You

The Extraordinary Within is more than just a self-help book; it's a guide to personal transformation. It will help you:

- **Unlock Your True Potential:** By following the seven steps outlined in this book, you'll be able to break free from self-imposed limitations and tap into your extraordinary abilities.
- **Achieve Your Goals:** With practical strategies and real-life examples, you'll be equipped to set, pursue, and achieve even your most ambitious goals.
- **Create Lasting Change:** This book will empower you to make lasting changes in your life, changes that lead to a more fulfilling, successful, and extraordinary existence.

- **Inspire Others:** As you grow and achieve success, you'll be in a position to inspire and uplift those around you, creating a ripple effect of positive change in your community and beyond.

Embark on Your Journey

As you turn the pages of this book, you're not just reading —you're embarking on a journey. A journey to discover the extraordinary within you, to challenge the status quo, and to achieve the impossible. The path won't always be easy, but with the guidance and strategies in this book, you'll be prepared to navigate the challenges and celebrate the victories.

The time to unlock your potential is now. Let this book be your guide as you step into the extraordinary future that awaits you.

| one |

Step 1: Discovering Your Hidden Potential

Understanding Your Strengths: Recognize Your Unique Strengths and Talents

Discovering your hidden potential begins with understanding and embracing your strengths. You may have been conditioned to focus on your weaknesses, often thinking, "I'm a terrible speaker," "I'm a horrible friend," or "I'm the worst cleaner." This can be even more challenging if you grew up in an environment where everything you did was criticized by family members. Such criticism can lead you to see nothing positive about yourself, making it difficult to recognize your strengths or hidden potential. People tend to voice these perceived shortcomings even before others notice, which can hold them back from succeeding. Recognizing even just one thing you are good at is the first step to discovering the extraordinary within you.

1

Strengths and It's Impact

Strengths are the consistent, near-perfect performance of an activity. They encompass both inherent talents and skills developed over time through practice and experience. Strengths allow individuals to perform at their best and are integral to achieving success. Embracing your strengths is crucial to unlocking your hidden potential and achieving extraordinary outcomes.

When I first began working as a case manager in the mental health field, one of my primary tasks was conducting a "strengths-based assessment." This comprehensive evaluation focuses on an individual's talents, skills, education, and social resources, rather than solely on their mental illness or challenges. This strengths-based mindset counters the stereotype that people with mental health issues lack strength. Recognizing and building on strengths is a core principle in mental and behavioral health. To truly know ourselves and our capabilities, we must acknowledge our successes, both past and present, and use this awareness to enhance our skills and improve our weaknesses.

None of us want to be surrounded by people who only see the worst in us, yet we often do this to ourselves. This self-criticism prevents us from seeing how extraordinary we are, especially for perfectionists. Perfectionists often believe nothing is ever good enough, always finding something to tweak. They might say, "Her dress needed a touch to be perfect," or "He spoke well but could have rephrased the introduction." These irrational expectations mean they never feel satisfied, despite receiving praise from others.

To recognize our strengths, we must accept that things don't have to be perfect—they just need to be good enough. Start by noticing the small things you do well every day or ask loved ones to point out your strengths. Those who care about us often see us more clearly than we see ourselves. Remember, the focus is on strengths, not weaknesses. Recognizing your unique strengths and talents is the first step in discovering your hidden potential. Many people go through life without truly understanding what they are good at or what makes them unique, leading to unfulfilled potential and a lack of direction.

To identify your strengths, start by reflecting on your past experiences. Think about times when you felt particularly successful or proud of your accomplishments. What activities were you engaged in? What skills did you use? Asking friends, family, or colleagues for feedback can also provide valuable insights into your strengths.

As John Wooden wisely said, *"Don't let what you cannot do interfere with what you can do."* By embracing this mindset, we can begin to unlock our hidden potential and discover the extraordinary within ourselves.

Example:

Consider someone who is naturally skilled at organizing and leading teams. Despite these strengths, they focus on their perceived inability to speak publicly, which undermines their confidence. By recognizing and developing their organizational talents, they could take on leadership roles that play to their strengths rather than avoiding opportunities due to a focus on their weaknesses.

Research on Strengths:

Research suggests that people who use their strengths regularly are more likely to be engaged and satisfied with their lives. According to a study by the Gallup Organization, individuals who focus on their strengths are six times more likely to be engaged in their jobs and three times more likely to report an excellent quality of life.

Many people spend their lives trying to fit into molds created by others—whether it's societal expectations, familial pressures, or professional demands. Often, in trying to conform to these external standards, we lose sight of what makes us unique. Understanding your strengths is the process of peeling back these layers and reconnecting with your core capabilities.

For example, someone who uses the Gallup Strengths-Finder assessment to identify their top strengths might discover that they excel in areas like strategic thinking or relationship building. Armed with this knowledge, they can pursue careers that align with these strengths, such as project management or sales, rather than careers that emphasize areas where they are weaker.

Reflective Question:

- What strengths have you overlooked in your life, and how can you start to leverage them?

Examples of Strengths:

- Empathy: The ability to understand and share the feelings of others.
- Analytical Thinking: The ability to systematically and logically work through complex issues.
- Leadership: The ability to guide and inspire others toward a common goal.
- Creativity: The capacity to generate innovative ideas and solutions.
- Resilience: The ability to recover quickly from setbacks and adapt to change.

Practical Application:

Someone who identifies leadership as a strength might pursue a role that allows them to mentor and lead teams, such as a management position. By focusing on this strength, they can excel and make a significant impact in their organization.

Reflective Question:

- How can you apply your strengths in your current job or personal life to achieve better results?

Talents and It's Impacts

Talents are natural abilities or aptitudes that individuals are born with. They are innate tendencies that come effortlessly and can be developed into strengths with practice and application. Research suggests that while talents are inherent, their full potential is realized through deliberate practice and development. Anders Ericsson's research on deliberate practice highlights that talent provides a foundation, but sustained effort and practice are crucial for achieving high levels of expertise. Carol Dweck's work on the growth mindset underscores the idea that talents can be cultivated through dedication and hard work.

Real-Life Scenario:

Consider a person who has a natural talent for verbal communication. This talent might lead them to excel in roles that require strong communication skills, such as teaching or public relations. With practice, they can turn this talent into a strength, enhancing their effectiveness in these roles.

Reflective Question:

- Which of your natural talents have you developed into strengths, and how have they benefited you?

Examples of Talents:

- Musical Talent: A natural ability to understand, create, or perform music.
- Athletic Talent: Innate physical abilities that contribute to superior performance in sports.
- Artistic Talent: A natural aptitude for visual arts, such as drawing, painting, or sculpting.
- Verbal Talent: An inherent skill in using language effectively for communication.
- Mathematical Talent: An intuitive grasp of numerical concepts and problem-solving.

Recognizing Your Unique Strengths and Talents

- **Self-Reflection:** Start by dedicating time to introspection. Recall moments in your life when you felt genuinely fulfilled and in the zone. What activities were you engaged in during those times? What specific skills or traits did you exhibit? Write these down as they will form the foundation of your strengths profile.
- **Seek Feedback:** Sometimes, our strengths are more apparent to others than to ourselves. Engage with trusted friends, family members, and colleagues. Ask them about times when they saw you excel or make a significant impact. Their observations can provide valuable insights that you might have overlooked.
- **Strengths Assessment Tools:** Utilize tools like the Clifton Strengths (formerly StrengthsFinder) assessment, which is designed to help individuals identify

their top strengths. This tool is based on extensive research and can offer a structured approach to understanding your unique capabilities.

- **Identify Patterns:** Look for recurring themes in your reflections and feedback. Do specific skills or attributes appear repeatedly? These patterns are indicative of your core strengths.

- **Document Your Strengths:** Create a comprehensive list of your strengths and talents. This document will serve as a reference point as you navigate through this book and embark on your journey of personal growth.

Building and Developing Strengths and Talents

Strategies to Build and Develop Strengths:

- **Identify Your Strengths:** Use assessments like CliftonStrengths to identify your top strengths. Reflect on your past successes and seek feedback from others to gain insights into your strengths.

- **Focus on Strengths:** Concentrate on leveraging and developing your strengths rather than trying to improve weaknesses. Engage in activities and roles that allow you to use your strengths regularly.

- **Continuous Learning:** Invest in continuous learning and skill development related to your strengths. Attend workshops, take courses, and seek mentorship to enhance your abilities.

- Set Strength-Based Goals: Set specific, measurable, achievable, relevant, and time-bound (SMART) goals that align with your strengths. This approach will help you maximize your potential and achieve better outcomes.

- **Seek Feedback:** Regularly seek feedback on your performance to identify areas for improvement and refine your strengths. Constructive feedback helps you stay on track and make necessary adjustments.

Reflective Question:

- What steps can you take to further develop your strengths this year?

Strategies to Build and Develop Talents:

- **Identify Natural Talents:** Reflect on activities that come naturally to you and bring you joy. Seek input from others who can recognize your natural abilities.

- **Engage in Deliberate Practice:** Follow Anders Ericsson's principles of deliberate practice by engaging in focused, goal-oriented practice. Break down complex skills into smaller components and practice them systematically.

- **Cultivate a Growth Mindset:** Embrace Carol

Dweck's growth mindset by believing that talents can be developed through effort and perseverance. View challenges as opportunities to grow and improve.

- **Find Role Models:** Identify individuals who excel in areas where you have natural talents. Study their approaches, seek mentorship, and learn from their experiences to enhance your own abilities.
- **Create a Supportive Environment:** Surround yourself with people who support and encourage your talent development. Join communities, clubs, or groups that provide opportunities for practice and growth.
- **Set Stretch Goals:** Challenge yourself with stretch goals that push you beyond your current capabilities. These goals should be ambitious yet attainable, providing a sense of accomplishment as you progress.

Reflective Question:

- Which talent will you focus on developing further, and what steps will you take?

Growth Mindset: Embracing Limitless Potential and Thinking Ahead

A growth mindset is the belief that abilities, intelligence, and talents can be developed through dedication, effort, and a willingness to learn. This concept, introduced by psychologist Carol Dweck, contrasts with a fixed mindset, which is the belief that abilities are innate and unchangeable—you either have them, or you don't. Having a growth mindset involves embracing challenges, persevering through obstacles, and seeing effort as the path to mastery. It's about recognizing that growth and improvement are always possible, regardless of your starting point.

A key aspect of adopting a growth mindset is having the courage to be a beginner. It requires the willingness to step out of your comfort zone and tackle new challenges, even when success is not guaranteed. This mindset acknowledges that learning is a process, and it's okay to not be perfect from the start. It's about focusing on progress rather than perfection, understanding that each step forward, no matter how small, contributes to your overall growth.

Working in the mental health field has shown me firsthand how vital it is to embrace this mindset. The caseload and exposure to the traumatic experiences of others can be overwhelming. Despite these genuine difficulties, I chose not to limit myself by believing that my abilities were finite. Instead, I embraced the belief that my abilities were limitless, understanding that while the work would be hard, I had what it took to succeed in my field. Some people might become defeated by the sheer thought of the workload, believing there is no way they can manage it. However, sometimes you need to test your abilities to discover how extraordinary you truly are. Often, we fail to achieve the impossible because we fail to try.

Closely tied to the concept of the growth mindset is *forward thinking*, which focuses on future planning and the anticipation of change. Forward thinking complements a growth mindset by encouraging individuals and organizations to proactively look ahead, set goals, and make strategic decisions that align with their future vision. While a growth mindset emphasizes continuous development, forward thinking provides the roadmap by asking, "What's next?" and "How can I prepare for future challenges?"

For example, in the mental health field, professionals who adopt forward thinking alongside a growth mindset will continuously look for ways to improve their coping mechanisms, expand their knowledge base, and anticipate future challenges in their work. This allows them to not only survive but thrive in a demanding field by aligning their long-term goals with a mindset that fuels personal and professional growth. By refusing to see setbacks as roadblocks and instead embracing them as learning opportunities, forward-thinking individuals can maintain the resilience needed to continue advancing their careers and personal development.

In the larger context of personal and professional growth, forward thinking takes the principles of a growth mindset and applies them to long-term goals. Just as those with a growth mindset understand that improvement requires effort and time, forward thinkers recognize the importance of planning and preparation for future success. In a business or personal context, forward thinking is vital for anticipating challenges, preparing for changes, and continuously evolving.

On a personal level, forward thinking encourages individuals to look beyond immediate obstacles and keep their long-term vision in mind, using setbacks as opportunities to learn and grow. A growth mindset ensures that they do not get discouraged by temporary failures, while forward thinking provides the strategic framework to keep moving toward their desired future. Together, a *growth mindset* and *forward thinking* create a powerful combination, empowering individuals and organizations to not only face challenges but thrive by staying committed to learning and proactively preparing for the future.

Example of a Growth Mindset:

Naomi's story is a testament to the power of the growth mindset. During one of our family summer vacations, she faced a challenge at a trampoline park where she had to climb three bouncing obstacles in succession without falling. Despite multiple failures, she refused to give up. She eventually conquered the obstacles through persistence and a willingness to adapt her strategy. This experience demonstrated her belief that she could improve with effort and perseverance—a core principle of the growth mindset.

By embracing a growth mindset, you permit yourself to

explore your full potential. It's about testing your limits, pushing beyond perceived barriers, and discovering just how extraordinary you truly are. This mindset not only enhances personal development but also has a positive impact on how we approach challenges in all areas of life.

Reflective Question:

- In what areas of your life can you apply a growth mindset to overcome challenges?

The Power of the Growth Mindset:

Embracing a growth mindset transforms the way we approach challenges and setbacks.

Here are some of the core principles of a growth mindset:

- **Challenges as Opportunities:** Instead of avoiding difficult tasks, approach them with curiosity and a willingness to learn. Challenges become opportunities to expand your skills and knowledge.
- **Persistence in the Face of Setbacks:** When encountering obstacles, remember that persistence is key to overcoming them. Every setback is a step toward mastery.

- **Effort as a Path to Mastery:** Understand that effort is crucial to success. Talent alone is not enough; dedication and hard work are essential for growth.
- **Learning from Criticism:** Constructive criticism is valuable feedback that can help you improve. Embrace feedback as a tool for growth rather than a personal attack.
- **Inspiration from Others:** Rather than feeling threatened by the success of others, use it as inspiration. Learn from their strategies and apply those lessons to your own journey.

Reflective Question:

- How can you shift your mindset to view challenges as opportunities for growth?

Cultivating a Growth Mindset:

To cultivate a growth mindset, practice the following strategies:

- Reframe Challenges: Instead of seeing challenges as threats, view them as opportunities to learn and grow. Remind yourself that every difficulty you face is a chance to improve.
- Embrace Failure: Understand that failure is not a reflection of your worth but a part of the learning process.

Analyze your failures to understand what went wrong and how you can do better next time.

- Value Effort: Recognize and celebrate the effort you put into your tasks, regardless of the immediate outcome. Effort is a critical component of growth and success.
- Seek Feedback: Actively seek feedback from others and use it to guide your improvement. Constructive criticism is a valuable tool for growth.
- Adopt a Learning Mindset: Approach every situation with a desire to learn. Whether it's a new project at work or a personal challenge, focus on what you can learn from the experience.

Reflective Question:

- What specific actions can you take to cultivate a growth mindset in your daily life?

Overcoming the Hedonic Treadmill: Cultivating True Contentment and Internal Growth

As you journey toward a growth mindset, it's essential to recognize that true contentment comes from within, rather than from external achievements. The concept of the *hedonic treadmill* explains why; despite overcoming significant challenges or reaching major milestones, our happiness often returns to a baseline level. This understanding reinforces the importance of developing inner resilience and finding joy in personal growth, rather than constantly seeking external validation.

To break free from the cycle of the hedonic treadmill, we must focus on practices that nurture our inner selves. *True contentment* is not about the constant pursuit of more, but about appreciating the present moment and the intrinsic value of our experiences. Here are some practical ways to cultivate this mindset, rooted in both practical actions and biblical wisdom:

1. **Practice Gratitude Daily**: Start each day by reflecting on what you are grateful for. Keeping a gratitude journal helps you focus on the positives in your life, shifting your mindset from what you lack to what you have. The Bible reminds us in *1 Thessalonians 5:18*, "Give thanks in all circumstances; for this is God's will for you in Christ Jesus." Gratitude is a key to finding contentment in every situation.

2. **Focus on Spiritual Growth**: Dedicate time each day for prayer, meditation, and reading Scripture. This cultivates a deeper relationship with God, which is the foundation for true contentment. As *Matthew 6:33* encourages, "But seek first his kingdom and his righteousness, and all these things will be given to you as well." Prioritizing your spiritual life ensures that your contentment is rooted in God's presence rather than in worldly achievements.

3. **Serve Others**: Engage in acts of service, whether

through volunteering, helping a neighbor, or simply offering a kind word. Serving others shifts the focus from yourself and fosters a sense of fulfillment. *Acts 20:35* tells us, "It is more blessed to give than to receive." Serving others brings joy and purpose, enhancing your sense of contentment.

4. **Cultivate Humility**: Regularly reflect on your life and acknowledge both your strengths and your limitations. Accepting yourself as you are, and striving to grow humbly, leads to deeper contentment. *James 4:10* teaches us, "Humble yourselves before the Lord, and he will lift you up." Humility reminds us that our value is not in what we achieve, but in who we are in Christ.

5. **Embrace Simplicity**: Simplify your life by decluttering your physical and mental spaces. Focus on what truly matters and let go of the pursuit of unnecessary material possessions or status. As *Matthew 6:19-20* advises, "Do not store up for yourselves treasures on earth... But store up for yourselves treasures in heaven." Simplicity helps us focus on eternal values over material wealth.

6. **Practice Contentment in the Present**: Learn to find peace in the present moment, rather than constantly striving for the next achievement. Mindfulness and being fully present in daily activities help cultivate this mindset. *Philippians 4:11* echoes this, "I have learned to be content whatever the circumstances." Contentment is a skill that can be developed, regardless of external conditions.

7. **Trust in God's Plan**: When faced with challenges, remind yourself that God has a plan for your life. Surrendering control and trusting in God's wisdom can bring profound peace. *Jeremiah 29:11* assures us, "For I know the plans I have for you, declares the Lord, plans to prosper you and not to harm you, plans to give you hope and a future." Trusting in God's plan allows us to find contentment in His care and guidance.

By integrating these practices into your daily life, you not only counter the effects of the hedonic treadmill but also build resilience and a deeper sense of contentment. Recognizing that true joy comes from within—through personal growth, spiritual fulfillment, and meaningful connections—frees you from the endless pursuit of external validation and enables you to embrace the extraordinary within you.

Discovering Your Hidden Potential: Understanding Your Strengths

Activity 1: Strengths Inventory

Objective: Recognize and articulate your unique strengths and talents.

Instructions:

Self-Reflection: Spend 15 minutes writing down

activities you enjoy and excel at. Consider both professional and personal contexts.

Feedback Collection: Ask five trusted friends, family members, or colleagues to share what they believe are your top strengths. Compare their feedback with your self-assessment.

Strengths Mapping: Create a visual map or list combining your self-reflection and feedback. Highlight recurring strengths.

Assessment:

Strengths Inventory Chart: Document your top 10 strengths based on self-reflection and external feedback.

Reflection Questions:

- Which strengths surprised you the most?

_____

- How do these strengths align with your current goals and activities?

_____

- How can you leverage these strengths more effectively in your daily life?

Solutions:

Strengths-Based Planning: Integrate your strengths into your daily tasks and long-term goals. For example, if you have strong organizational skills, apply them to manage projects efficiently.

Skill Development: Identify areas where you can further develop your strengths. For instance, if creativity is a strength, consider taking a course to enhance your creative skills.

Embracing a Growth Mindset

Activity 2: Developing a Growth Mindset

Instructions:

Identify Limiting Beliefs: List any opposing thoughts or beliefs you have about your ability to handle setbacks or failures.

Reframe Beliefs: For each limiting belief, write down a positive, growth-oriented alternative. For example, replace "I always fail at new things" with "I learn and grow from every new experience."

Practice Affirmations: Create a list of positive

affirmations based on your reframed beliefs. Repeat these affirmations daily to reinforce a growth mindset.

Activity 3: Growth Mindset Journaling

Objective: Develop the belief that abilities can be developed through dedication and hard work.

Instructions:
Daily Reflections: Keep a journal to reflect on daily experiences, focusing on challenges and how you approached them.

Mindset Shifts: Write about moments where you faced setbacks and how you can view them as opportunities for growth.

Affirmations: Create a list of growth mindset affirmations to repeat daily. Examples include "I learn from my mistakes" and "Challenges help me grow."

Assessment:
Journaling Review: Review your journal entries after one month. Identify patterns in your thinking and areas where you've applied a growth mindset.

Growth Mindset Quiz: Take an online growth mindset

assessment (such as Carol Dweck's Mindset Quiz) to evaluate your progress.

Solutions:

Mindset Reinforcement: Regularly revisit and update your growth mindset affirmations. Please post them in visible places to remind yourself daily.

Learning Opportunities: Seek out opportunities to challenge yourself and learn new skills. Enroll in courses, join groups, or take on new projects that push your boundaries.

Conclusion of Step 1:

Discovering your hidden potential is the foundation for all future growth and success. By identifying your strengths and embracing a growth mindset, you set the stage for unlocking the extraordinary capabilities within you. This journey is about understanding that your abilities are not static but can be developed and expanded through continuous learning, perseverance, and the cultivation of inner resilience.

As you apply these principles to your life, you'll begin to recognize that true contentment and fulfillment come from within, not from external achievements. By integrating practices such as gratitude, spiritual growth, and service to others, you build a strong foundation that will support you in every aspect of your life. This first step is just the beginning of a journey toward achieving the impossible, providing you with the essential tools to start recognizing and harnessing your potential. Embrace this process, and you'll discover that the path to success is not only possible but within your reach, paving the way for remarkable achievements.

Next Step Reference:

In the next step, we will explore how to overcome limiting beliefs, transform negative thoughts, and build the confidence needed to pursue your goals with determination. This process is essential for breaking free from self-imposed limitations and realizing your true potential.

| two |

Step 2: Overcoming Limiting Beliefs, Thoughts and Building Confidence

Understanding Beliefs and Their Impact on Individuals

B eliefs are the convictions or acceptances that certain things are true or real. They are mental representations and attitudes that individuals hold about themselves, others, and the world around them. These beliefs are formed through personal experiences, cultural and societal influences, education, and the opinions of others, and they significantly shape behavior and decision-making. Understanding how these beliefs form and influence our behavior is the first step toward overcoming them.

In my practice as a therapist, I encounter people from all walks of life who present with various mental health challenges, including depression and anxiety. Many of these individuals have formed negative self-beliefs and automatic thoughts based on their experiences. Previously, experts believed that people with depression or anxiety developed negative thinking patterns because of their condition. However, psychologists now recognize that these negative thoughts may contribute to the development of depression and anxiety.

This concept is linked to cognitive distortions—biased or irrational thoughts that distort the way a person perceives themselves, their life, specific day-to-day situations, relationships, and other people. These distortions can contribute to mental health conditions such as depression and anxiety. For example, someone might believe that "no one likes me," leading to a fear of social situations. This belief can cause them to avoid social interactions, which in turn increases their feelings of loneliness and depression, further reinforcing the belief that they are unlikable. This negative cycle perpetuates their mental health issues.

Common Cognitive Distortions:

1. **All-or-Nothing Thinking (Black-and-White Thinking):** Viewing situations in extreme, absolute terms, such as seeing things as all good or all bad, with no middle ground.
2. **Overgeneralization:** Making broad interpretations from a single or few events, such as believing that one negative experience means that everything will go wrong.

3. **Catastrophizing:** Expecting the worst possible outcome or seeing a situation as far worse than it actually is.

4. **Mental Filtering:** Focusing only on the negative aspects of a situation while ignoring the positives.

5. **Jumping to Conclusions:** Making negative interpretations without actual evidence. This includes mind-reading (assuming others think negatively of you) and fortune-telling (predicting a negative outcome without evidence).

6. **Emotional Reasoning:** Believing that your feelings reflect reality, such as thinking "I feel it, therefore it must be true."

7. **"Should" Statements:** Using "should," "must," or "ought" statements to set unrealistic expectations for oneself or others, leading to feelings of guilt or frustration.

To learn more about cognitive distortions, check out the additional resources at the end of the book.

Disclaimer: If you or a loved one is facing mental health challenges such as depression, or anxiety, or have thoughts of suicide, please seek immediate consultation with a mental health counselor or professional who can provide support tailored to your specific needs.

The Power of Thoughts:

Thoughts are the cognitive processes that occur in our minds as we interpret and make sense of our environment and experiences. They encompass a wide range of mental activities, including reasoning, remembering, problem-solving, and reflecting. Our perceptions, emotions, beliefs, and past experiences can influence thoughts.

The Bible also speaks to this truth. The book of Proverbs illustrates the power of thoughts and their impact on one's life and perspective. Proverbs 23:7 says, "For as he thinks in his heart, so is he." This scripture emphasizes that our thoughts shape our identity, behavior, and, ultimately, our reality. Negative thoughts can lead us down a path of despair and self-doubt, while positive, God-centered thoughts can transform our lives, guiding us towards fulfillment and peace.

The thoughts you hold, particularly negative ones, have the power to affect your emotions and behaviors significantly. For example, if you believe that no one likes you, you may begin to fear social situations, assuming that others don't have your best interests at heart. This fear may lead you to avoid social interactions, which in turn can make you feel more depressed and anxious. This withdrawal reinforces your belief that no one likes you without recognizing that your actions are contributing to this cycle. This negative loop exacerbates depression or anxiety, making it crucial to reframe and challenge these beliefs.

In my work with clients, I help them identify and process

negative core beliefs or automatic negative thought patterns that contribute to their depression or anxiety. Through evidence-based modalities like cognitive-behavioral therapy, we dig deeper into the origins of these beliefs and thoughts. This process allows individuals to uncover their true selves and break free from limiting beliefs.

It's important to note that therapy or counseling is not a quick-fix solution; it takes time and practice. Some individuals may have underlying issues, such as trauma or severe mental health conditions, that contribute to their negative thoughts or beliefs. These deeper issues may require further exploration to help the individual truly feel better. Each person's journey is unique and requires a personalized approach.

Positive vs. Negative Thoughts

- **Positive Thoughts**: Constructive and optimistic, these thoughts focus on what can go right, the potential for success, and the positives in any situation. They foster a sense of hope, motivation, and resilience. Examples include: "I can handle this challenge" and "I am capable and resourceful."
- **Negative Thoughts**: Destructive and pessimistic, these thoughts focus on potential failures, negatives in any situation, and self-doubt. They can lead to feelings of hopelessness, anxiety, and depression. Examples include: "I will fail no matter what" and "I'm not good enough."

Positive Realistic Thoughts vs. Just Positive Thoughts

- **Positive Realistic Thoughts**: Optimistic yet grounded in reality, these thoughts acknowledge challenges and obstacles but maintain a constructive outlook and focus on actionable solutions. For example: "This project is challenging, but I have the skills and resources to handle it."

- **Just Positive Thoughts**: Overly optimistic, these thoughts may ignore potential difficulties or unrealistic expectations. While they can boost morale temporarily, they might not prepare individuals for real-world challenges. For example: "Everything will be perfect."

Relationship Between Thoughts and Beliefs

Beliefs act as a filter through which thoughts are generated. For example:

- **Belief**: "I am capable and competent."
- **Positive Thought**: "I can overcome this obstacle."
- **Belief**: "I am not good enough."
- **Negative Thought**: "I will fail at this task."

Beliefs can reinforce thought patterns, and repeated thoughts can, in turn, reinforce beliefs. This cyclical relationship means that altering one's beliefs can lead to changes in thought patterns and vice versa.

Evidence-Based Insights

Cognitive-behavioral therapy (CBT) is an evidence-based approach that highlights the connection between thoughts, beliefs, and behaviors. CBT interventions often focus on identifying and modifying dysfunctional beliefs to change negative thought patterns, demonstrating the impact of beliefs on thoughts and overall mental health.

Overcoming Limiting Beliefs and Embracing Your Potential

Recognizing your strengths and talents is crucial for achieving success, but this process can be significantly hindered by limiting beliefs. These self-imposed barriers convince you that you are not capable, not deserving, or not enough. Overcoming these beliefs is essential for unlocking your full potential and ensuring that your goals and vision are aligned with your true capabilities. However, changing limiting beliefs can be particularly challenging, especially when they've been ingrained in your mind for years. These negative thoughts are often intertwined with your self-identity, making them difficult to overcome.

For me, overcoming limiting beliefs required letting go of the narrative I had clung to for so long: "I'm just a boy from the slums of West Point, Liberia, who gave his parents hell as a teenager and made many mistakes." This belief kept me anchored to my past, defining myself by my failures and shortcomings. But to grow, I had to embrace a new belief:

"My past does not define who I am, and I have the power to rewrite my inspiring future."

This inner critic—the voice that tells you you're not worthy, not good enough, or a failure due to past experiences or mistakes—can be relentless. These are the battles you fight daily, and ultimately, the only person who can rescue you from these thoughts is yourself. You must reach a point where you say, "I'm tired of believing these lies—these limiting thoughts and beliefs that have been holding me down." It's essential to recognize that you are more than your mistakes, errors, or setbacks. What you have inside is more than enough; it's extraordinary.

As I began to reshape my mindset, I often thought that if I only had the opportunity to go to the United States, I could get the quality education needed to pursue my purpose or calling. This belief in the power of education and knowledge, combined with my humble beginnings, played a significant role in my ability to rise above life's challenges. Education became more than just a goal; it was a lifeline, a way to break free from the limitations of my past and carve out a path toward success and fulfillment.

US Navy SEAL David Goggins describes two levels of belief. The first is the surface-level belief preached by others, such as "Believe in yourself" or "You can do it." While well-intentioned, this level of belief often lacks the depth needed to sustain you through life's toughest challenges. The second level, however, is born through resilience—the belief that comes from working your way through multiple pains, hardships, and trials. Despite everything, you keep pushing forward, refusing to quit, until you reach a point where you almost give up, only to realize a hidden potential within you that you never knew existed.

I understand this second level of belief very well because I have been there. As a young immigrant boy, leaving my homeland of Liberia and coming to a foreign land, I was filled with self-doubt and fear of disappointing my family. I carried the weight of my family's expectations, with advice from family members—including those who doubted my success—constantly ringing in my ears, urging me not to disappoint or disgrace them. I worried every day, but I refused to let these fears hold me back. Instead, I transformed them into something extraordinary. It was a struggle deeply rooted within me, invisible to others but very real to me.

Many times, I had to put a smile on my face and pretend that everything was okay, even when it wasn't. Yet, despite my challenges, I was determined not to let them define me. Belief is about finding that one small thing within you and holding onto it, no matter how insignificant it may seem. It's not about what you don't have, but about what you do have, even if it's just a tiny spark of hope or optimism.

Practicing self-compassion is crucial in this journey. Treat yourself as you would treat your best friend, with kindness and understanding, because here's the truth: everyone makes mistakes, and that's what it means to be human. My journey has taught me that belief is more than just words of encouragement from others; it's about discovering and holding onto that inner strength within you, especially when faced with trials. This inner strength, fueled by a deep belief in your potential and a commitment to your goals will push you through obstacles and help you focus on your purpose.

By overcoming these limiting beliefs and embracing your potential, you can unlock a life of purpose, growth, and fulfillment.

Impact of Beliefs on Individuals

- **Behavior and Actions:** Beliefs directly influence an individual's behavior and actions. For example, if someone believes they are capable of achieving a goal, they are more likely to take steps toward it.
- **Emotional Responses:** Beliefs shape how people perceive and respond to events emotionally. Positive beliefs can lead to feelings of confidence and happiness, while negative beliefs can cause anxiety and sadness.
- **Decision-Making:** Beliefs play a crucial role in the decision-making process. They act as filters through which people evaluate options and make choices.
- **Interpersonal Relationships:** Beliefs about oneself and others affect how individuals interact in their relationships. For instance, believing in the goodness of people fosters trust and cooperation.

Empowering Beliefs vs. Limiting Beliefs

Empowering Beliefs: Empowering beliefs are positive convictions that inspire confidence, motivation, and action. They enhance an individual's ability to achieve their goals and improve their overall well-being.

Examples of Empowering Beliefs:

- "I am capable of achieving anything I set my mind to."
- "Every challenge is an opportunity to learn and grow."
- "I am deserving of success and happiness."
- "With hard work and dedication, I can overcome any obstacle."
- "I have the resources and support I need to succeed."

Limiting Beliefs: Limiting beliefs are negative convictions that restrict potential and hinder progress. They create mental barriers that prevent individuals from pursuing their goals and realizing their full potential.

Examples of Limiting Beliefs:

- "I am not good enough."
- "I will never be able to achieve my goals."
- "Success is only for others, not for me."
- "I am destined to fail."
- "I don't have what it takes to be successful."

Transforming Limiting Beliefs into Empowering Beliefs

Steps to Transform Beliefs:

1. **Identify Limiting Beliefs:** Reflect on your thoughts and identify beliefs that are holding you back. Write them down to make them concrete.
2. **Challenge the Beliefs:** Question the validity of your

limiting beliefs. Ask yourself, "Is this belief based on facts or assumptions? What evidence contradicts this belief?"

3. **Reframe the Beliefs:** Replace limiting beliefs with empowering ones. For example, change "I am not good enough" to "I am capable and continually improving."

4. **Affirm the New Beliefs:** Reinforce your empowering beliefs through positive affirmations. Regularly remind yourself of your new beliefs to embed them in your mindset.

5. **Take Action:** Act in alignment with your new empowering beliefs. Small actions taken consistently will reinforce these beliefs and help you build momentum.

Groupthink and Its Impact on Beliefs

C ertain beliefs, however, have the potential to prevent us from succeeding in life. Common beliefs I've encountered include, "This job is not for people like us," "No one will ever recognize us, so why try?" or "I am not good enough." Beliefs like these are not just wrong but disabling. Once ingrained, they have the power to hold you back, but you also have the power to change them and even prove them wrong.

Some of us have been programmed to believe outright wrong and misleading things, either due to our past experiences or the experiences of others. This is especially true when it comes to "groupthink"—the phenomenon where the beliefs of the group we belong to affect how we think about certain things, even if we haven't experienced them. Multiple studies have shown that the collective beliefs of a group can significantly influence an individual's mindset and behavior.

Groupthink, a term coined by social psychologist Irving Janis, refers to the psychological phenomenon where the desire for harmony or conformity within a group results in irrational or dysfunctional decision-making. The pressure to align with the group can suppress dissenting opinions and critical thinking, leading individuals to adopt beliefs or make decisions they might disagree with independently.

One of the key impacts of groupthink is its ability to shape and reinforce collective beliefs within a group, even if those beliefs are unfounded or detrimental. For instance, Janis's research highlighted how groupthink can lead to poor decision-making in high-pressure environments, where the desire to maintain group cohesion overrides the consideration of alternative viewpoints. This effect is not limited to organizational settings; it can also influence personal beliefs and behaviors within social groups.

By recognizing the power of groupthink and actively working to counteract it, you can begin to challenge and change the disabling beliefs that may be holding you back. Whether in professional settings or personal life, it's essential to cultivate a mindset that values critical thinking and the courage to challenge the status quo when necessary. This approach not only guards against the negative impacts of groupthink but also empowers individuals to break free from limiting beliefs and achieve their full potential.

When you become aware of the limiting beliefs that have taken root in your mind and make a conscious effort to challenge and change them, you begin to unlock your true potential. It's about recognizing that you have more power and capability than you've been led to believe. This shift in belief—rooted in resilience and strengthened through overcoming challenges—is the key to recognizing the extraordinary within.

Overcoming Resistance to Growth

In the journey toward cultivating a growth mindset, one common challenge is the internal resistance to change, known as *psychological reactance*. This occurs when individuals perceive that their freedom to choose or control their behaviors is being threatened. When someone is told they must change or that a particular way of thinking is wrong, it often triggers a defensive response, making them cling more strongly to their existing beliefs.

This phenomenon can be a significant barrier to embracing a growth mindset. For example, when we are encouraged to adopt new ways of thinking or to view challenges as opportunities for growth, our initial reaction might be to resist these ideas, especially if they contrast sharply with our established beliefs or self-identity.

Understanding psychological reactance can help in managing this resistance. Rather than viewing growth as something imposed from the outside, it can be reframed as a personal choice that empowers you to achieve your full potential. By recognizing and acknowledging the natural tendency to resist change, you can consciously work to overcome it, thus allowing yourself to embrace new perspectives and opportunities for development.

Incorporating this understanding into your mindset allows you to navigate the discomfort of change and use it as a stepping stone toward growth. This is where self-awareness and reflective practices become essential tools in your journey, helping you to identify when reactance is at play and how to move beyond it.

Self-Awareness and Reflective Practices:

To effectively manage psychological reactance and foster a growth mindset, it is important to engage in self-awareness and reflective practices. These strategies can help you recognize when resistance is hindering your progress and provide insight into how to move past it. Here are some reflective questions to guide you:

1. What are some situations where I've felt an instinctive resistance to advice or suggestions? What emotions did I experience during those moments?
2. How do I typically react when someone challenges my beliefs or opinions? Do I become defensive, or am I open to considering alternative perspectives?
3. Can I recall a time when I resisted a change or idea, only to later realize its value? What influenced my initial resistance, and how did my perspective shift over time?
4. Are there specific areas of my life where I tend to experience more psychological reactance? What underlying fears or concerns might be driving this resistance?
5. How can I create a mindset that balances my desire for autonomy with an openness to new ideas and constructive feedback?

Engaging with these questions encourages introspection

and helps you identify patterns in your reactions. Understanding these patterns allows you to recognize when psychological reactance is at play, giving you the power to make more informed decisions about how to respond. This self-awareness is key to overcoming unnecessary resistance and opening yourself up to growth and new opportunities.

By consciously addressing and managing psychological reactance, you can transform resistance into a catalyst for growth, ultimately leading to a more resilient and adaptable mindset. This approach not only enhances personal development but also strengthens your ability to embrace change and thrive in the face of challenges.

Challenging Self-Doubt

S elf-doubt is a pervasive obstacle that can hinder personal growth and achievement. It often manifests as negative beliefs about oneself, stemming from past experiences, societal pressures, or internal comparisons with others. Overcoming self-doubt begins with identifying these limiting beliefs and transforming them into empowering perspectives.

This tendency is closely tied to imposter syndrome, a well-documented phenomenon in psychology where self-doubt and the fear of being exposed as fraud limit our potential. Interestingly, even highly skilled and knowledgeable individuals experience this feeling of inadequacy.

But why do capable people feel inadequate? The answer lies in our natural inclination to doubt ourselves, which can limit our potential.

Evidence-Based Research on Self-Doubt

Studies have shown that moderate self-doubt can encourage better preparation and more thorough work, leading to improved performance. For example, research published in the *Journal of Personality and Social Psychology* found that individuals who experience some levels of self-doubt are often more motivated to double-check their work and seek out additional resources, leading to higher-quality outcomes. On the other hand, excessive self-doubt can be paralyzing, preventing individuals from taking risks or pursuing opportunities that could lead to success.

Recognizing and addressing self-doubt is crucial for personal and professional growth. By transforming self-doubt into a tool for improvement rather than a barrier to success, you can unlock your full potential and achieve extraordinary results.

To identify and challenge self-doubt, start by:

- **Self-Reflection:** Take time to reflect on moments when you've felt unsure or critical of yourself. What thoughts or beliefs triggered these feelings? Write them down to gain clarity.
- **Patterns and Triggers:** Notice recurring themes or situations where self-doubt arises. Are there specific triggers—such as deadlines, new challenges, or social interactions—that intensify these feelings?
- **External Influences:** Consider how societal expectations, cultural norms, or comparisons with others contribute to your self-doubt. Recognize that these influences may not accurately reflect your true capabilities.

Practical Application:

For example, a common workplace scenario might involve someone believing they are not good enough for a promotion. By identifying this belief, challenging it with evidence of past successes, reframing it into a more positive statement, and then acting on it (such as applying for the promotion), they can overcome this limiting belief and potentially achieve the career advancement they desire.

Reflective Question:

- *Take a moment to write down a limiting belief you hold about yourself and list three pieces of evidence that contradict this belief.*

Building Self-Confidence

Self-confidence is the belief in your abilities to achieve goals and navigate life's challenges effectively. It's not just an inherent trait but a mindset that can be cultivated through intentional practices and positive self-reinforcement. By consistently recognizing your strengths and accomplishments and facing challenges with resilience, you can develop a deep-seated confidence that empowers you to take on new opportunities and overcome obstacles.

A critical aspect of building true self-confidence is understanding who you are. For those who follow Christ, this begins with understanding your identity in Him. The foundation of self-confidence and self-esteem is often rooted in recognizing who we are in God's eyes. The Bible teaches that as children of God, we are loved, accepted, and valued by our Heavenly Father (John 1:12; Romans 8:15-17). When we grasp our worth in Christ, it transforms how we see ourselves—worthy, capable, and cherished.

Renewing your mind is another key to cultivating self-confidence. Romans 12:2 encourages us to transform our thoughts by regularly reading and meditating on God's truth. The Scriptures are filled with powerful affirmations of our identity in Christ. By focusing on these truths, we can replace negative, self-defeating thoughts with positive, God-centered ones, which strengthens our confidence.

Moreover, being confident in God's love is essential. The Bible assures us that God's love for us is unconditional and unchanging (Romans 8:38-39). When we truly understand and accept this love, it becomes the bedrock of our self-confidence and self-esteem. This divine love reassures us that we are never alone and that we have the strength and support to face any challenge.

For those who do not identify with any religious affiliation, building self-confidence can start with recognizing the things that make your life meaningful. What specific practices, values, or relationships give your life purpose and direction? If you struggle to identify what makes your life meaningful, consider exploring the benefits that spirituality or religious practices might offer. Research has shown that religion can provide valuable benefits, including a sense of purpose, meaning, and social cohesion.

For instance, studies indicate that individuals with a strong sense of religious or spiritual identity often experience higher levels of self-esteem and well-being. A study published in the *Journal of Religion and Health* found that people who regularly participate in religious activities tend to have a greater sense of life satisfaction and resilience. The sense of community, moral framework, and connection to something greater than oneself can contribute significantly to one's overall sense of confidence and well-being.

Research Insights on Self-Confidence

Research indicates that self-confidence is crucial for mental health, personal achievement, and social interactions. Some key findings include:

- **Performance and Achievement**: High self-confidence is linked to better performance in academic, professional, and athletic domains. Confident individuals are more likely to set ambitious goals and persist in the face of obstacles.
- **Mental Health**: Self-confidence is associated with lower levels of anxiety and depression. It promotes resilience and helps individuals cope with stress more effectively.
- **Social Interactions**: Confident individuals tend to have better social relationships. They are more likely to engage in social activities, communicate effectively, and build supportive networks.

Low and High Self-Confidence

Low Self-Confidence

Low self-confidence is characterized by a lack of trust in one's abilities and judgment. Individuals with low self-confidence may experience:

- **Self-Doubt**: Persistent questioning of one's skills and decisions.
- **Fear of Failure**: Avoidance of challenges due to fear of making mistakes.
- **Negative Self-Image**: A poor view of oneself, leading to feelings of worthlessness.
- **Impact on Behavior**: Hesitation to take risks, difficulty in asserting oneself, and avoidance of new opportunities.

High Self-Confidence

High self-confidence involves a strong belief in one's abilities and a positive self-image. However, excessively high self-confidence can lead to overconfidence, which may result in:

- **Overestimation of Abilities**: Underestimating challenges and overestimating one's capacity to handle them.
- **Risk-Taking**: Engaging in risky behaviors without adequate preparation or consideration.
- **Dismissal of Feedback**: Ignoring constructive criticism leads to stagnation and potential failure.

Maintaining a Healthy Balancing of Self-Confidence

Maintaining a healthy balance in self-confidence is essential for optimal functioning and well-being. This involves regularly reflecting on your strengths and weaknesses to realistically understand your capabilities while acknowledging areas for improvement. It's important to establish achievable and challenging goals, breaking larger tasks into smaller, manageable steps to build confidence gradually. Embrace setbacks as opportunities to learn and grow by developing a growth mindset that values effort and improvement over perfection. Encourage constructive feedback from trusted sources and use it to refine your skills and knowledge. Practice self-compassion by treating yourself with kindness and understanding, recognizing that everyone makes mistakes and experiences setbacks. Continuously build your skills and knowledge in areas that matter to you, as competence enhances confidence. Finally, maintain an optimistic yet realistic outlook by focusing on what you can control and preparing for challenges with a proactive mindset.

Research Insights on Balancing Self-Confidence

Research findings underscore the importance of balanced self-confidence. Studies indicate that moderate levels of self-confidence are associated with the best outcomes in terms of performance, mental health, and social relationships.

Overconfidence and under-confidence can both hinder personal and professional growth.

For instance, a study published in the *Journal of Personality and Social Psychology* found that individuals with moderate self-confidence are more likely to achieve their goals compared to those with either low or excessively high self-confidence. This is because they are realistic about their capabilities, open to learning, and resilient in the face of challenges.

By understanding the dynamics of self-confidence and implementing strategies to maintain a healthy balance, individuals can optimize their potential, enhance their well-being, and achieve sustainable success.

Ways to Build Self-Confidence

- **Celebrate Your Strengths**: Take inventory of your strengths, talents, and past accomplishments. Celebrate your successes—no matter how small—to build a foundation of self-esteem.
- **Goal-Setting**: Set realistic and achievable goals that align with your values and aspirations. Accomplishing these goals reinforces your belief in your capabilities and strengthens your confidence.
- **Visualization**: Visualize yourself succeeding in challenging situations or achieving your long-term goals. Visualization techniques help create a mental image of success, which can enhance confidence and motivation.

- **Competence through Experience**: Gain competence in areas that matter to you through practice and experience. As you develop skills and overcome obstacles, your confidence naturally grows.

Embracing a Growth Mindset for Confidence

As discussed in **Step 1**, a growth mindset is the belief that abilities and intelligence can be developed through dedication and hard work. It encourages resilience, learning from setbacks, and a focus on continuous improvement—all of which are essential for building lasting self-confidence.

Conclusion of Step 2

Overcoming limiting beliefs, transforming negative thoughts, and building self-confidence are foundational steps in unlocking your full potential. Understanding how beliefs and thoughts influence your actions and decisions empowers you to take control of your mindset, reframe limiting beliefs, and cultivate empowering ones.

This journey begins with self-awareness—recognizing the beliefs and thoughts that have held you back. It involves challenging those beliefs, reframing them into empowering statements, and reinforcing your newfound beliefs through consistent action. Along the way, it's essential to remain mindful of psychological reactance—the internal resistance that can arise when confronted with change. By understanding this phenomenon, you can navigate your natural defenses and embrace growth with a more open and flexible mindset.

Furthermore, be aware of the impact of groupthink on your beliefs and decisions. Groupthink can subtly influence you to conform to the ideas of the majority, even when those ideas don't align with your true self or goals. By fostering critical thinking and the courage to challenge the status quo, you can avoid the pitfalls of groupthink and stay true to your values and aspirations.

Remember, the journey to building confidence and overcoming self-doubt is not a one-time event but a continuous practice of resilience, self-reflection, and growth. As you move forward, take these principles to heart: believe in your ability to grow and adapt, focus on positive and realistic thoughts, and use your inner strength to push through challenges. By doing so, you are not just overcoming obstacles; you are laying the foundation for a future filled with possibilities and success.

Next Step Reference:

In the next step, we will explore how to further solidify your newfound confidence by identifying your purpose, setting meaningful goals, and crafting a vision that aligns with your true potential. This ongoing journey of self-discovery and growth will empower you to achieve the extraordinary.

| three |

Step 3: Identifying Purpose, Goal Setting, and Vision Crafting

Purpose: The "Why" Behind Your Existence

Purpose can be defined as the overarching reason for your existence—the "why" behind everything you do. It is deeply personal and unique to each individual. Unlike goals, which are specific and time-bound, purpose is a life-long guiding principle that shapes your decisions and influences your actions across all areas of your life. Purpose serves as the foundation that gives your goals meaning and direction. Without a clear sense of purpose, even well-defined goals can feel empty or unfulfilling. Identifying your purpose involves reflecting on what truly matters to you, what drives you, and what you hope to achieve in the long run. This deeper understanding of your motivations can guide you in setting goals that are not only realistic but also deeply aligned with your values and aspirations.

Purpose is often linked to your values, passions, and the impact you want to make on the world. It is not something that is always immediately apparent; instead, it is discovered through self-reflection, exploration, and the pursuit of meaningful experiences.

Key Questions for Identifying Purpose:

- What are my core values?
- What do I want to contribute to the world?
- What activities or accomplishments bring me the most satisfaction?
- How do my goals align with my long-term vision for my life?

Purpose, Mission, and Vision: The Foundation of Extraordinary Success

Purpose isn't just about reaching a specific goal; it applies to every aspect of your life. It is the driving force behind your actions and decisions, and it needs to be authentic. Purpose is an internal quest—an ongoing journey rather than a destination. It is intentional, looking ahead with a clear sense of direction, and it can be cultivated over time.

The more you understand who you are and what you want, the less you allow external circumstances to upset or bother you. Research shows that having a sense of purpose serves as a buffer against daily challenges and stressors.

Despite the inevitable difficulties in life, purpose provides resilience. It's important to note that purpose is a subjective experience, not something that can be objectively measured. Yet, it has been shown to contribute positively to well-being and even predict longevity.

Dr. Martin Luther King Jr.'s "I Have a Dream" speech is a powerful example of what purpose looks like in action— clear, focused, and deeply connected to a greater cause. Similarly, Viktor Frankl, in his book *Man's Search for Meaning*, emphasizes that even in the face of immense trials, such as surviving a concentration camp, the key was not merely to survive, but to understand "why" one wanted to survive. This underscores the power of purpose in sustaining us through the most challenging circumstances.

My purpose was clear early in my life: to help others. Proverbs 19:21 says, "Many are the plans in a person's heart, but it is the Lord's purpose that prevails." This verse illustrates that, while we may have many plans, it is our deeper purpose that ultimately guides us. Purpose is not a destination; it is a journey that often requires refinement and fine-tuning. You don't reach a point where you say, "I have accomplished my purpose," because it is a continuous work in progress.

As a young man growing up in Liberia, I valued education and believed it was the key to a brighter future. Despite my clear understanding of my purpose to help others, my goals were not very clear. I initially pursued a degree in nursing, but it took me two years to realize that nursing wasn't the right path for me. My purpose began to take shape during a conversation with my wife when I realized I wanted to work in the mental and behavioral health field. Once this became clear, I crafted specific goals: "I want to pursue a degree in Psychology," followed by actionable objectives: "I will apply for the Psychology program."

This experience taught me that without clear goals, fulfilling your purpose can be difficult, if not impossible. Jeremiah 29:11—"For I know the plans I have for you," declares the Lord, "plans to prosper you and not to harm you, plans to give you hope and a future"—reminds us that our purpose is part of a larger plan that leads to growth and fulfillment.

Psychologist Anthony Burrow explains that purpose isn't something to be found; it's something we can develop from within. Purpose is an active process, not a passive one. It evolves as we grow, face challenges, and gain new insights. In his research, Dr. Burrow identified several pathways to purpose:

Pathways to Purpose:

1. **Gradual Development:** Purpose often emerges gradually as we pursue passions or hobbies.
2. **Response to Life Events:** Purpose can emerge in response to major life events, such as caring for a loved one or reinventing yourself after a job loss.
3. **Inspiration from Others:** Observing someone with a strong sense of purpose can inspire you to develop your own.

Purpose isn't static; it grows and evolves as we do. It's cultivated through our actions, our choices, and the way we respond to life's challenges. By identifying and embracing your purpose, you create a foundation that guides your goals, shapes your vision, and drives your actions. This sense of purpose will sustain you, buffer you from stress, and ultimately contribute to a fulfilling and meaningful life.

The Importance of Purpose

Having a clear sense of purpose is associated with numerous benefits, including:

- **Enhanced Motivation**: Purpose provides a compelling reason to persevere through challenges and setbacks. When you know why you're doing something, you're more likely to stay committed to your goals.
- **Increased Resilience**: Purpose gives you the strength to overcome obstacles and bounce back from failures. It acts as a source of inner strength during difficult times.
- **Improved Well-Being**: Research shows that individuals with a strong sense of purpose experience higher levels of happiness, satisfaction, and overall well-being. Purpose contributes to a sense of fulfillment and contentment in life.
- **Greater Focus and Clarity**: Purpose helps you prioritize your time and energy on what truly matters.

It provides clarity in decision-making and reduces distractions.

- **Stronger Relationships**: Purpose often involves contributing to something larger than yourself, whether it's your community, family, or society as a whole. This fosters deeper connections and a sense of belonging.

Emotional Intelligence: The Key to Purposeful Goal Setting

In your journey to identifying purpose, setting goals, and crafting a vision, Emotional Intelligence (EQ) is a critical component in recognizing and harnessing your extraordinary potential. It involves the ability to understand and manage your emotions, as well as the emotions of others, which is essential for personal growth, effective leadership, and professional success. The concept of EQ, popularized by psychologist Daniel Goleman, encompasses several core elements: self-awareness, self-regulation, motivation, empathy, and social skills. Together, these components influence how individuals manage behavior, navigate social complexities, and make personal decisions that lead to positive outcomes. This skill is not just about managing emotions but using them effectively to solve problems, communicate, and navigate life's challenges.

Understanding Emotional Intelligence

Emotional Intelligence includes several key components:

1. **Self-awareness**: Recognizing and understanding your emotions, and how they influence your thoughts and actions. Self-awareness is crucial for setting goals that align with your true passions and values.

2. **Self-regulation**: The ability to manage your emotions,

particularly in stressful or challenging situations. This includes thinking before acting, which is vital when pursuing long-term goals that require patience and perseverance.

3. **Motivation**: Harnessing your emotions to stay driven and focused on your goals. Motivation in EQ is about being resilient and optimistic, even in the face of set-backs.

4. **Empathy**: Understanding the emotions of others and considering their perspectives. Empathy helps in building meaningful relationships and networks, which are essential when crafting a vision that involves collaboration and support.

5. **Social Skills**: Building and maintaining relationships, communicating effectively, and managing conflicts. Strong social skills ensure that you can work effectively with others to achieve your goals.

The Role of Emotional Intelligence in Goal Setting

Emotional Intelligence is fundamental in setting and achieving goals because it influences how you perceive your abilities, manage stress, and interact with others. High EQ helps you set realistic and meaningful goals, stay committed to them, and navigate the emotional ups and downs that come with pursuing a vision.

The Bible also underscores the importance of managing emotions and acting with wisdom. For example, Proverbs 15:18 states, "A hot-tempered person stirs up conflict, but the one who is patient calms a quarrel." This verse high-lights the value of self-regulation—a key component of EQ—in maintaining harmony and achieving success.

Applying Emotional Intelligence to Your Life

To fully harness the power of Emotional Intelligence in your goal-setting journey:

- Practice mindfulness to become more aware of your emotions and how they impact your decisions.
- Engage in active listening to improve empathy and strengthen your relationships.
- Develop resilience by focusing on motivation and self-regulation, especially when facing challenges.

By cultivating Emotional Intelligence, you enhance your ability to identify your true purpose, set aligned goals, and craft a vision that is both inspiring and achievable. EQ not only supports personal growth but also equips you to lead others, make wise decisions, and navigate the complexities of life with grace and confidence.

Mission and Vision: Aligning Purpose with Action

While purpose is your "why," your mission is your "what." Your mission defines what you intend to achieve and the steps you will take to get there. It is your purpose in action. A robust vision, on the other hand, is the mental image of what success looks like when you are fulfilling your mission. Your vision is the aspirational endpoint that guides your daily actions and long-term goals.

In his book *Start with Why*, Simon Sinek highlights the power of identifying your "why" as the foundation for both personal and professional success. According to Sinek, the "why" represents your core purpose, the driving force behind your actions and decisions. Your mission, or the "what," defines the specific goals and steps you'll take to bring your purpose to life. Meanwhile, your vision is the aspirational image of success when you fulfill your mission.

Together, these elements create a clear and motivating framework that guides your daily actions and long-term objectives, ensuring that everything you do is aligned with your deeper sense of purpose. When you understand your "why," your mission and vision gain clarity and meaning. This alignment not only drives your actions but also inspires others to join you on your journey, amplifying the impact of your efforts.

Understanding and integrating your "why" into your

mission and vision can transform how you approach your goals, leading to a more purposeful and fulfilling life.

How to Identify Your Purpose

Identifying your purpose is a journey of self-discovery that requires introspection, exploration, and patience. Here are some steps to help you uncover your purpose:

- **Reflect on Your Values and Passions**

Your values and passions are critical indicators of your purpose. Start by asking yourself questions like:

- What do I value most in life?
- What activities or causes am I most passionate about?
- When do I feel most fulfilled and energized?
- What principles guide my decisions and actions?

Write down your answers and look for common themes. These can provide valuable clues about your purpose.

Example: If you value helping others and feel most passionate when volunteering, your purpose may involve making a positive impact on people's lives.

Consider Your Strengths and Talents

Reflect on the following:

- What are my natural strengths and abilities?
- What tasks or activities do I excel at?
- What feedback have I received from others about my strengths?

By aligning your strengths with your passions, you can identify a purpose that leverages your unique abilities.

Example: If you have a talent for communication and a passion for social justice, your purpose might involve advocating for marginalized communities.

Explore Meaningful Experiences: Reflect on past experiences that have had a profound impact on you:

- What experiences have shaped my beliefs and values?
- What challenges have I overcome, and how did they influence me?
- What moments in my life have felt most significant?

These experiences can reveal your purpose by highlighting the areas of life that resonate most deeply with you.

Example: If overcoming a personal health challenge inspired you to pursue a healthcare career, your purpose may be to help others achieve wellness.

Think About the Impact You Want to Make: Ask yourself:

- What impact do I want to have on the world?

- How do I want to be remembered?
- What legacy do I want to leave behind?

By considering the impact you want to make, you can identify a purpose that aligns with your desire to create positive change.

Example: If you want to leave a legacy of environmental conservation, your purpose may involve advocating for sustainable practices.

- **Embrace Curiosity and Experimentation** Purpose is not always immediately apparent, and it's okay to explore different paths. Embrace curiosity and be open to experimenting with new experiences, roles, and activities.

Example: By volunteering in various community organizations, you may find that your true passion lies in education, leading you to pursue a career in teaching.

Overcoming Obstacles to Purpose

Identifying and living out your purpose can be challenging. Common obstacles include:

- **Fear of Failure**: The fear of failing can prevent you from pursuing your purpose. Remember, purpose is a journey, not a destination.
- **External Pressures**: Societal expectations or financial

concerns can make it difficult to focus on your purpose. Stay true to yourself and prioritize what matters most to you.

- **Lack of Clarity**: You may feel uncertain about your purpose. This is normal, and it's essential to give yourself time to explore and reflect.
- **Comparisons to Others**: Comparing yourself to others can lead to self-doubt. Your purpose is unique to you, and it's okay to follow your path.

Cultivating a Purpose-Driven Life

Once you've identified your purpose, the next step is to cultivate a purpose-driven life. Here are some strategies:

- **Align Your Actions with Your Purpose** Ensure your daily actions are aligned with your purpose.

Example: If your purpose is to promote mental health awareness, prioritize activities such as volunteering with mental health organizations.

- **Surround Yourself with Supportive People** Surround yourself with people who support your purpose.

Example: Join a group or organization that aligns with your purpose, such as a professional association or volunteer group.

- **Practice Mindfulness and Reflection** Regularly practice mindfulness and reflection to stay connected to your purpose.

Example: Set aside time each day for meditation or journaling to reconnect with your purpose.

- **Adapt and Evolve** Be open to adapting your purpose as you grow and change.

Example: If you discover new passions, consider how they might influence your purpose.

- **Share Your Purpose with Others** Sharing your purpose with others can inspire them to find their purpose.

Example: Mentor someone who is on their journey of self-discovery or speak about your purpose at events.

Goal Setting: SMART Goals and Their Importance

Goals are specific, measurable, achievable, relevant, and time-bound (SMART) objectives that individuals set to accomplish within a particular timeframe. They provide a clear direction and framework for action, helping individuals focus their efforts and resources toward achieving desired outcomes.

Research supports the effectiveness of goal setting in

enhancing performance and motivation. A study published in the American Journal of Lifestyle Medicine found that individuals who set specific goals were more likely to achieve their desired outcomes than those who did not.

Examples of Goals:

- Career Goal: Obtain a promotion to a managerial position within two years.
- Fitness Goal: Run a marathon in six months.
- Educational Goal: Complete a master's degree in three years.
- Financial Goal: Save $10,000 for a down payment on a house within one year.

Understanding SMART Goals:

SMART goals are Specific, Measurable, Achievable, Relevant, and Time-bound. They provide a clear direction and framework for action, helping individuals focus their efforts and resources toward achieving desired outcomes.

SMART Goals Example:

- **Specific:** "I will read one book on personal development each month for the next six months to enhance my knowledge in this area."
- **Measurable:** "Save $10,000 for a down payment on a house within one year."
- **Achievable:** "Run a marathon in six months by following a structured training program."
- **Relevant:** "Pursue a certification in project management to advance my career."
- **Time-bound:** "Complete my master's degree in three years."

The Importance of Goal Setting:

Research shows that individuals who set SMART goals—Specific, Measurable, Achievable, Relevant, and Time-bound—are more likely to achieve success compared to those with vague or poorly defined objectives. A study by Locke and Latham highlights the effectiveness of goal-setting theory in enhancing performance and motivation across various domains.

- **Enhanced Focus**: SMART goals provide clarity and direction, guiding your efforts toward specific outcomes. By defining precisely what you want to achieve, you can prioritize tasks and allocate resources effectively.
- **Increased Motivation**: Clear goals create a sense of purpose and motivation. They give you something concrete to strive for, boosting your commitment and persistence in pursuing your aspirations.
- **Measurable Progress**: With quantifiable criteria, you can track your progress and celebrate milestones along the way. This reinforces your sense of accomplishment and encourages continuous improvement.
- **Accountability and Commitment**: Setting SMART goals holds you accountable for your actions. It encourages self-discipline and commitment to follow through on your plans, even when faced with challenges or setbacks.

Setting Realistic Goals:

Setting realistic goals is crucial for success. Unrealistic goals can lead to frustration and failure, while realistic goals, adjusted based on experience, provide a clear pathway to achievement.

Activity 1: Setting SMART Goals

Objective: To help readers create Specific, Measurable, Achievable, Relevant, and Time-bound goals.

Instructions:

Reflect on a personal or professional goal you want to achieve.

Break down the goal using the SMART criteria.

Worksheet:

Goal: _____

Specific: What exactly do you want to achieve?

_____

Measurable: How will you measure your progress and know when you've achieved your goal?

_____

Achievable: Is your goal realistic and attainable? What steps will you take to achieve it?

_____

Relevant: Why is this goal important to you? How does it align with your broader objectives?

Time-bound: What is your deadline for achieving this goal? What milestones will you set along the way?

Example:

Goal: Improve public speaking skills to advance in my career

Specific: I want to deliver a presentation confidently at the annual company meeting.

Measurable: I will track the number of practice sessions and seek feedback from peers.

Achievable: I will join a public speaking group and practice weekly.

Relevant: Enhancing my public speaking skills will help me lead projects and gain visibility in my organization.

Time-bound: I will deliver the presentation at the annual company meeting in six months.

Solution:

To ensure goals are well-defined, encourage readers to review their goals periodically and adjust them as needed. Setting intermediate milestones can help maintain motivation and track progress.

Activity 2: Developing a Goal Achievement Plan

Objective: Create a detailed plan with actionable steps to achieve a specific goal.

Instructions:

Select one of your **SMART** goals.

Outline the steps required to achieve this goal.

Identify potential obstacles and strategies to overcome them.

Assign deadlines for each step and track your progress.

Worksheet:

Goal: _____

Step 1: What is the first action you need to take?

_____

Deadline:

_____

Step 2: What is the following action you need to take?

_____

Deadline:

_____

Step 3: What resources or support do you need?

_____

Deadline:

_____

Step 4: What obstacles might you encounter, and how will you address them?

_____

Deadline:

_____

Step 5: How will you measure your progress and stay motivated?

_____

Deadline:

_____

Solution:

Regularly review and update your goal achievement plan.

Celebrate small victories along the way to maintain momentum. Seek feedback and support from mentors or peers to stay on track.

Activity 3: Goal Review and Adjustment

Objective: Regularly review and adjust your goals to ensure they remain relevant and attainable.

Instructions:

Schedule monthly goal review sessions.

Evaluate your progress on each goal.

Adjust your goals based on your progress and any changes in your circumstances.

Worksheet:

Goal:

_____

Progress: What progress have you made toward this goal?

_____

Challenges: What challenges have you encountered?

_____

Adjustments: What adjustments do you need to make to stay on track?

_____

Next Steps: What are your next steps to achieve this goal?

_____

Solution:

Regular reviews keep your goals aligned with your current situation and priorities. Adjusting goals ensures they remain realistic and attainable. Use feedback and self-reflection to make informed adjustments.

Creating a Roadmap: Developing Your Vision for Success

Once you've defined your SMART goals, the next step is to create a roadmap—a strategic plan that outlines actionable steps toward achieving your objectives. A clear vision acts as your guide, ensuring that you stay focused and aligned with your long-term aspirations.

- **Clarify Your Vision**: Start by vividly imagining your ideal future. What do you want to accomplish? How do you envision yourself growing and evolving? Your vision should be compelling and inspiring, reflecting your deepest desires and aspirations.
- **Define Long-term Objectives**: Break down your vision into long-term objectives that align with your values and priorities. These objectives serve as milestones along your journey towards achieving your ultimate goals.
- **Set Short-term Goals**: Identify actionable steps you can take in the short term to progress towards your long-term objectives. These smaller goals provide immediate direction and momentum, keeping you motivated and focused.
- **Create a Timeline**: Establish a timeline that outlines key milestones and deadlines for achieving each goal. A timeline helps you manage your time effectively and ensures consistent progress towards your vision.

Implementing Your Roadmap

- **Prioritize Tasks**: Determine the order of tasks based on their importance and urgency. Focus on high-priority activities that directly contribute to your goals.
- **Allocate Resources**: Identify the resources—such as time, money, and skills—needed to accomplish each task. Allocate these resources efficiently to maximize productivity and minimize obstacles.
- **Monitor Progress**: Regularly review your progress against the roadmap. Assess what's working well and where adjustments are needed. Stay flexible and adapt to changes as you navigate toward your goals.
- **Celebrate Achievements**: Acknowledge and celebrate milestones along the way. Celebrating your successes reinforces positive behaviors and motivates you to continue striving for excellence.

The Importance of Purpose, Goal Setting, and Vision Crafting

By integrating purpose into your goal-setting and vision-crafting processes, you create a robust framework for achieving personal and professional success. This approach ensures that your efforts are not only directed toward achievable goals but are also aligned with your deeper values and aspirations, leading to a more fulfilling and impactful life.

Realistic goal setting is a powerful process for envisioning your ideal future and motivating yourself to turn this vision into reality. By knowing precisely what you want to achieve, you can focus your efforts and resources effectively, paving the way for success.

Vision Crafting: Aligning Goals with Purpose and Values

What is a Vision?

A vision is a broad and inspiring statement that describes your long-term aspirations and desired future state. It acts as a guiding star that influences decision-making and goal-setting, providing a sense of purpose and direction.

Characteristics of a Vision:

- **Inspiring:** Motivates and energizes individuals to strive for a better future.
- **Future-Oriented:** Focused on long-term aspirations and outcomes.
- **Values-Based:** Reflects personal values, beliefs, and principles.
- **Holistic:** Encompasses various aspects of life, including career, personal growth, relationships, and well-being.

Examples of Vision Statements:

- Personal Vision: "To be a compassionate and impactful leader who inspires others to achieve their fullest potential."
- Career Vision: "To build a successful company that revolutionizes the renewable energy industry and promotes sustainability."
- Health Vision: "To live a balanced and healthy life, fostering physical, mental, and emotional well-being."
- Community Vision: "To create a supportive and inclusive community where everyone feels valued and empowered."

Importance of Having Clear Goals and Vision
For Personal and Professional Development

- Direction and Focus: Clear goals and vision provide a roadmap for where you want to go and what you want to achieve. They help prioritize actions and decisions, ensuring that efforts are aligned with desired outcomes.

- Motivation and Inspiration: A compelling vision inspires and motivates individuals to take action, even when faced with challenges. Goals break down the vision into manageable steps, providing a sense of accomplishment as each goal is achieved.
- Accountability and Measurement: Goals allow individuals to measure progress and hold themselves accountable. This ensures that they stay on track and make necessary adjustments to reach their vision.
- Resilience and Persistence: A strong vision and clear goals help individuals stay resilient in the face of setbacks. They provide a sense of purpose and motivation to persist through difficulties.
- Personal Growth and Fulfillment: Pursuing meaningful goals and a compelling vision leads to personal growth, self-discovery, and fulfillment. It allows individuals to realize their potential and live a purposeful life.

For Career and Business Success

- Strategic Planning: In a professional context, clear goals and vision are essential for strategic planning. They guide decision-making, resource allocation, and long-term planning.
- Team Alignment and Collaboration: A shared vision aligns team members and fosters collaboration. Clear goals provide a common focus and help teams work

together effectively towards achieving organizational objectives.

- Performance and Productivity: Goals enhance performance and productivity by providing clear targets and expectations. They enable employees to understand their roles and contributions to the organization's success.
- Innovation and Growth: A visionary mindset encourages innovation and continuous improvement. It challenges individuals and organizations to think creatively and explore new opportunities.
- Satisfaction and Retention: Employees who are aligned with an organization's vision and have clear goals are more satisfied and engaged. This leads to higher retention rates and a positive work environment.

Creating a Vision:

To create a compelling vision:

- **Visualize Your Ideal Future:** What do you want to accomplish? How do you see yourself growing and evolving?
- **Define Long-term Objectives:** Break down your vision into long-term objectives that align with your values and priorities.
- **Set Short-term Goals:** Identify actionable steps to progress toward your long-term objectives.

Bringing It All Together

To bring everything together, start by identifying your purpose—why you do what you do. From there, define your mission—what you want to achieve. Craft a vision that represents your ultimate success. Then, set specific goals that will guide your actions toward that vision. By understanding how purpose, mission, vision, and goals interconnect, you can visualize your path forward in a practical way, making it easier to stay focused and motivated on your journey.

This step is about aligning your inner motivations with external actions. It's about understanding who you are, what you want to achieve, and how you plan to get there. By following this process, you will not only create a roadmap for success but also ensure that your efforts are meaningful and deeply connected to your authentic self.

Activity 4: Creating a Vision Board

Objective: Help readers visualize their goals and create a roadmap for achieving them.

Instructions:
Gather materials such as magazines, printed images, scissors, glue, and a poster board.

Reflect on your long-term goals and aspirations.

Cut out images, words, and phrases that represent your goals and dreams.

Arrange and glue the cutouts onto the poster board to create a vision board.

Reflection Questions:
What themes or patterns do you notice in your vision board?

_____

_____

How do the images and words align with your SMART goals?

_____

_____

What steps will you take to turn your vision into reality?

_____

_____

Solution:

Creating a vision board helps clarify your goals and keep them in focus. Place the vision board in a prominent location to serve as a daily reminder of your aspirations. Regularly update the board as your goals evolve.

Activity 5: Vision Crafting Exercise

Objective: Develop a clear vision for your future and identify the steps needed to achieve it.

Instructions:

Find a quiet space and take a few deep breaths to center yourself.

Visualize your ideal life in detail. Where are you? What are you doing? Who are you with?

Write a detailed description of your vision.

Reflection Questions:

What emotions do you feel when envisioning your ideal life?

_____

_____

How does this vision align with your core values and goals?

_____

_____

What are the first steps you need to take to move toward this vision?

_____

_____

Solution:

Writing down your vision helps solidify it in your mind. Revisit and revise your vision as needed. Break down your vision into smaller, actionable steps and integrate them into your goal-setting plan.

Interactive Reflection:

- **Milestones and Resources:** What are the milestones you need to achieve along the way to your vision? What resources or support do you need to reach each milestone?
- **Alignment Check:** How do your current goals reflect

your core values? Are there any adjustments you need to make to ensure alignment?

Conclusion of Step 3

Identifying your purpose, setting SMART goals, and crafting a clear vision are essential components of both personal and professional growth. By establishing these foundational elements and developing a well-defined roadmap, you empower yourself to take proactive steps toward realizing your potential and achieving what may once have seemed impossible. Stay committed to your vision, grounded in your purpose, and view challenges as opportunities for growth. Celebrate each step of your journey as you move closer to extraordinary success.

Next Step Reference:

In the following step, we will delve into the practical strategies of time management, prioritization, and continuous learning. These skills are critical for maintaining momentum and staying focused on what truly matters in your journey to achieving the extraordinary.

| four |

Step 4: Time Management, Prioritization, and Continuous Learning

"TIME IS WHAT WE WANT MOST, BUT WHAT WE USE WORST." - WILLIAM PENN

Time management, prioritization, and continuous learning are critical elements for achieving extraordinary success. In today's fast-paced world, effectively managing your time, prioritizing tasks, and embracing lifelong learning are essential skills that allow you to focus on what truly matters and stay ahead in an ever-changing environment. This chapter provides comprehensive insights into these key areas, offering strategies and tools to help you unlock your full potential and achieve the seemingly impossible.

Time Management and Continuous Learning

A plan without proper time management will fail to

produce the desired results. The same is true for goals. Once you have identified your strengths, purpose, and goals, and crafted your vision, it is crucial to manage your time wisely. Effective time management significantly impacts how quickly and efficiently you can achieve your goals. You can often distinguish between those who plan well and manage their time effectively and those who do not by how long it takes them to achieve similar goals. A project that should take thirty minutes with good time management can stretch into hours or even days if unnecessary time is wasted.

Efficiency and Effectiveness

Two key concepts in time management are efficiency and effectiveness. Efficiency refers to performing tasks in the most economical way possible, minimizing waste, and maximizing output. Effectiveness, on the other hand, is about doing the right things—ensuring that your actions are aligned with your goals and purpose. Effective time management means not only doing things right but also doing the right things at the right time.

Understanding and mastering these two concepts—efficiency and effectiveness—will position you to navigate your resources and support systems more effectively, leading to long-term success and growth. However, it's essential to balance speed with quality. The concept of "moving fast and breaking things," popularized by Facebook CEO Mark Zuckerberg, emphasizes the importance of agility in innovation. Yet, without focusing on doing the right things effectively, this approach can lead to unintended consequences, such as compromising quality or breaking the wrong things.

Ultimately, the goal is not just to move fast, but to move fast with purpose. By mastering the balance between efficiency, effectiveness, and quality, you can achieve lasting success and create value in everything you do.

Effective Time Management: Strategies for Success

Time management involves organizing and planning how to allocate your time between specific activities. Effective time management enables you to work smarter, not harder, ensuring that you get more done in less time, even when time is tight, and pressures are high.

Strategies for Effective Time Management

- **Set Clear Goals:** Clearly defined goals give you direction and a sense of purpose.
- **Prioritize Tasks:** Identify the most important tasks and tackle them first. Use the Eisenhower Matrix to categorize tasks based on urgency and importance.
- **Create a Schedule:** Plan your day, week, or month in advance. Use tools like calendars, planners, or digital apps to keep track of your tasks.
- **Avoid Multitasking:** Focus on one task at a time. Multitasking can reduce productivity and the quality of your work.
- **Take Breaks:** Regular breaks improve focus and

productivity. The Pomodoro Technique, which involves working for 25 minutes and then taking a 5-minute break, can be effective.

- **Eliminate Distractions:** Identify and minimize distractions in your work environment. This could include turning off notifications, finding a quiet workspace, or using apps that block distracting websites.
- **Delegate Tasks:** Delegate tasks that others can do, freeing up your time for tasks that require your expertise.
- **Review and Adjust:** Regularly review your progress and adjust your plan as needed. Flexibility allows you to adapt to changing circumstances.

The Importance of Time Management

- **Increased Productivity:** Efficient time management helps you accomplish more in less time.
- **Reduced Stress:** Managing your time effectively can reduce the stress associated with deadlines and workloads.
- **Improved Focus:** Prioritizing tasks helps you focus on the most important activities.
- **Better Work-Life Balance:** Effective time management allows you to allocate time to personal activities and relationships.
- **Achieving Goals:** Time management is essential for setting and reaching personal and professional goals.

Prioritization: Focusing on What Matters Most

Prioritization involves determining the order in which tasks should be completed based on their importance and urgency. Effective prioritization ensures that you focus on tasks that have the most significant impact.

Importance of Prioritization

- **Focus on High-Impact Tasks:** Prioritization helps you focus on tasks that drive the most value and impact.
- **Avoid Burnout:** By focusing on what truly matters, you can avoid the stress and burnout that comes from trying to do everything at once.
- **Efficient Use of Resources:** Allocating time and resources to the most important tasks ensures efficiency.
- **Goal Achievement:** Prioritizing tasks aligned with your goals helps you achieve them more effectively.

Strategies for Prioritizing Tasks

- **Identify Key Tasks:** Determine which tasks are essential to achieving your goals.
- **Use the 80/20 Rule:** Also known as the Pareto Principle, this rule suggests that 80% of results come from 20% of efforts. Focus on tasks that yield the highest results.

- **Categorize Tasks:** Use the Eisenhower Matrix to categorize tasks into four quadrants:
- Urgent and Important: Do these tasks immediately.
- Important but Not Urgent: Schedule these tasks.
- Urgent but Not Important: Delegate these tasks if possible.
- Not Urgent and Not Important: Eliminate or defer these tasks.
- **Set Deadlines:** Establish deadlines for tasks to create a sense of urgency and importance.
- **Evaluate and Adjust:** Regularly review and adjust your priorities based on changing circumstances and new information.

Tools and Techniques for Prioritization

- **Eisenhower Matrix:** This tool helps categorize tasks based on their urgency and importance, aiding in effective prioritization.
- **ABC Method:** Categorize tasks into A (must-do), B (should-do), and C (nice-to-do) based on their priority.
- **MoSCoW Method:** Classify tasks into Must have, Should have, Could have, and Won't have to prioritize effectively.
- **Time Blocking:** Schedule high-priority tasks during your peak productivity hours to ensure they get done.
- **Daily Reviews:** Review your to-do list at the beginning and end of each day to adjust priorities as needed.

Prioritization Activities and Assessments

Daily Time Log:

Activity: Track how you spend your time over a week. Use a notebook or a time-tracking app to record all activities, including work, leisure, and sleep.

Assessment: At the end of the week, review your log to identify patterns. Note how much time you spend on productive activities versus distractions.

Solution: Adjust your schedule to reduce time spent on low-priority activities. For example, if you notice excessive time spent on social media, set specific limits or allocate that time to more productive tasks.

Prioritization Matrix:

Activity: Create a matrix with four quadrants: urgent and important, important but not urgent, urgent but not necessary, and neither urgent nor essential.

Assessment: Categorize your tasks into these quadrants.

Solution: Focus on tasks that are important but not urgent to prevent them from becoming urgent. Delegate or eliminate tasks that are neither urgent nor important.

Time Blocking:

Activity: Allocate specific blocks of time for different activities throughout your day. For example, dedicate morning hours to high-priority tasks and afternoons to meetings or routine tasks.

Assessment: At the end of the week, evaluate your productivity and adjust your blocks as needed.

Solution: Stick to your time blocks as closely as possible to create a structured and efficient routine.

Pomodoro Technique:

Activity: Use the Pomodoro Technique by working for 25 minutes, then taking a 5-minute break. After four sessions, take a more extended break of 15-30 minutes.

Assessment: Track your productivity during these sessions.

Solution: If you find specific tasks require more focus, extend your work periods to 45 or 60 minutes, followed by more extended breaks.

Continuous Learning: Staying Ahead in a Changing World

Continuous learning involves constantly expanding your knowledge and skills throughout your life. It is essential for personal development, adaptability, and staying competitive in today's rapidly changing world. This ongoing, voluntary pursuit of knowledge plays a crucial role in both personal and professional growth, keeping you adaptable and ready to face new challenges.

As you manage your time and prioritize your goals, you'll gain deeper insights into what works best for you and what doesn't. This is where continuous learning becomes vital. It requires an openness to feedback and criticism, which is essential for growth. However, this stage can be challenging; some people resist change and get stuck, while others thrive by staying flexible and open-minded.

Being open-minded doesn't mean accepting every suggestion or piece of advice indiscriminately. It involves critically assessing what aligns with your goals and values. As Henry Ford once said, *"Anyone who stops learning is old, whether at twenty or eighty. Anyone who keeps learning stays young."* An open mind allows you to adapt, make necessary changes, and seize opportunities that may not be perfect but are steps toward your ultimate goals.

Ultimately, continuous learning is about being purposeful and choosing the best possible options. As you work towards achieving your goals, you may not always get exactly what you want, but you may receive what is necessary to push you forward. It's about making wise decisions, not missing once-in-a-lifetime opportunities, and holding on to your core values.

Importance of Lifelong Learning

- **Adaptability:** Continuous learning helps you adapt to new challenges and changes in your personal and professional life.
- **Career Advancement:** Acquiring new skills and knowledge can lead to career growth and opportunities.
- **Personal Growth:** Learning new things fosters personal growth, satisfaction, and a sense of accomplishment.
- **Innovation:** Continuous learning encourages creativity and innovation by exposing you to new ideas and perspectives.
- **Resilience:** Knowledge and skills gained through continuous learning build resilience, enabling you to navigate difficulties effectively.

Strategies for Embracing Continuous Learning

- **Set Learning Goals:** Identify areas you want to improve or learn about. Set specific, achievable learning goals.
- **Leverage Online Resources:** Utilize online courses, webinars, and educational platforms like Coursera, Udemy, and LinkedIn Learning.
- **Read Regularly:** Read books, articles, and journals in your field to stay updated on the latest trends and knowledge.
- **Join Professional Organizations:** Participate in professional associations, workshops, and conferences to network and learn from peers.
- **Seek Feedback:** Regularly seek feedback on your performance and areas for improvement. Use this feedback to guide your learning efforts.
- **Experiment and Innovate:** Try new methods, techniques, or projects to apply what you've learned and gain practical experience.
- **Mentorship and Peer Learning:** Learn from mentors and peers. Engage in discussions, share knowledge, and collaborate on learning initiatives.

Tools and Techniques for Continuous Learning

- **Online Learning Platforms:** Use platforms like Coursera, edX, Udemy, and LinkedIn Learning for structured courses and certifications.
- **Reading Lists:** Maintain a list of books, articles, and journals relevant to your field. Make reading a daily habit.
- **Podcasts and Webinars:** Listen to industry podcasts and attend webinars to stay updated on current trends and insights.
- **Skill Development Workshops:** Participate in workshops and seminars to develop specific skills.
- **Professional Development Plans:** Create a personal development plan outlining your learning goals, strategies, and timelines.
- **Networking Events:** Attend industry events, conferences, and meetups to learn from others and share your knowledge.
- **Reflection and Journaling:** Reflect on your learning experiences and insights. Journaling helps consolidate knowledge and track progress.

Lifelong Learning Activities and Assessments

Personal Development Plan (PDP):

Activity: Create a PDP outlining your learning goals, the skills or knowledge you wish to acquire, and the resources or strategies you will use.

Assessment: Review your progress quarterly to ensure you are on track.

Solution: Adjust your plan as needed, incorporating new learning opportunities and setting realistic timelines for achieving your goals.

Learning Journal:

Activity: Maintain a journal where you record new insights, skills learned, and reflections on your learning experiences.

Assessment: Review your journal entries monthly to track your progress and identify areas for improvement.

Solution: Use your reflections to guide your future learning activities and address any challenges you encounter.

Online Courses and Workshops:

Activity: Enroll in online courses or attend workshops relevant to your field or interests.

Assessment: Complete course evaluations and apply what you've learned to real-world scenarios.

Solution: Select courses that offer practical applications and opportunities for hands-on learning.

Reading and Research:

Activity: Dedicate time each week to reading books, articles, or research papers related to your interests or career.

Assessment: Summarize critical takeaways and how they can be applied to your personal or professional life.

Solution: Join book clubs or discussion groups to enhance understanding and gain different perspectives.

Solutions to Common Challenges to Lifelong Learning

Procrastination:

Solution: Break tasks into smaller, manageable steps. Use techniques like the Pomodoro Technique to maintain focus and motivation. Set deadlines for each step to create a sense of urgency.

Overwhelm:

Solution: Use the prioritization matrix to focus on high-impact tasks. Delegate tasks when possible and break large projects into smaller, more manageable parts.

Distractions:

Solution: Identify common distractions and create strategies to minimize them. This might include setting specific times for checking emails and social media, creating a designated workspace, and using productivity apps to block distracting websites.

Lack of Motivation:

Solution: Set clear, achievable goals and celebrate small wins. Find a learning community or accountability partner to keep you motivated and engaged. Remind yourself of the long-term benefits of continuous learning.

By implementing these activities and assessments, you can enhance your time management, prioritization, and continuous learning skills. These strategies will help you stay organized, focused, and adaptable, paving the way for achieving extraordinary success.

Conclusion for Step 4:

Effective time management, prioritization, and continuous learning are essential skills essential for achieving success. Mastering these skills not only enhances your ability to reach your goals but also helps you cultivate the mindset and relationships needed to recognize your extraordinary potential and achieve what might have once seemed impossible.

By focusing on time management and prioritization, you can concentrate on what truly matters, making significant strides toward your objectives. Embracing lifelong learning ensures you remain adaptable, innovative, and competitive in an ever-changing world. Together, these strategies create a powerful framework for personal and professional growth, enabling you to unlock your extraordinary potential and achieve the impossible.

Next Step Reference:

In the next step, we will explore the importance of networking, mentorship, and support systems. These elements are crucial for personal and professional growth, providing the guidance and opportunities needed to sustain your progress and continue on the path to success.

| five |

Step 5: Networking, Mentorship, and Support Systems

"EVERYONE YOU WILL EVER MEET KNOWS SOME-
THING YOU DON'T."
— *BILL NYE*

In today's interconnected world, the significance of networking, mentorship, and support systems is paramount. These elements are vital for both personal and professional development, offering guidance, opportunities, and a reliable safety net. This chapter explores the value of mentors, the process of building meaningful connections, and strategies for expanding and nurturing your support network. By understanding and utilizing these resources, you can unlock new levels of potential and achieve extraordinary outcomes.

The Power of Networking: Building Connections for Success

Networking is about establishing and nurturing relationships that provide mutual support, information, and opportunities. Effective networking opens doors to new opportunities, offers valuable insights, and helps you achieve your goals. Building a diverse network ensures you have access to a broader range of perspectives and support, making you better equipped to face challenges and seize opportunities.

Importance of Networking

- **Access to Opportunities:** Networking can lead to job offers, partnerships, and collaborations that you might not have encountered otherwise.
- **Knowledge Sharing:** Through networking, you can gain insights and information from others in your field, keeping you updated on industry trends and best practices.
- **Support System:** A strong network provides emotional and professional support during challenging times.
- **Visibility and Reputation:** Networking helps you establish your presence and reputation in your industry or community.
- **Career Development:** Many career advancements come through connections and recommendations from within your network.

Strategies for Effective Networking

- **Be Authentic:** Authenticity is key in building genuine connections. Be yourself and show genuine interest in others.
- **Be Prepared:** Have a clear understanding of your goals and what you offer. This helps you communicate effectively during networking opportunities.
- **Leverage Online Platforms:** Utilize social media platforms like LinkedIn to connect with professionals in your industry. Share valuable content and engage with others' posts.
- **Attend Events:** Participate in industry conferences, workshops, and networking events. These provide opportunities to meet like-minded individuals.
- **Follow Up:** After meeting someone, follow up with a personalized message to reinforce the connection. This could be through email, a LinkedIn message, or a phone call.

Building a Diverse Network

A diverse network can provide a broader range of perspectives, opportunities, and support. Here's how to build and maintain a diverse network:

- **Expand Your Horizons:** Don't limit your network to people within your immediate field or industry. Connect with individuals from various backgrounds and industries.
- **Seek Out Different Perspectives:** Engage with people who have different experiences, skills, and viewpoints. This can provide valuable insights and innovative ideas.
- **Be Inclusive:** Make an effort to include and support individuals from underrepresented groups. This fosters a more inclusive and supportive network.
- **Nurture Relationships:** Building a diverse network requires ongoing effort. Regularly engage with your connections through meaningful interactions.

Finding and Nurturing Mentorship Relationships

Mentors play a pivotal role in personal and professional development. A mentor is someone who offers knowledge, advice, and support based on their own experiences. They help you navigate challenges, identify opportunities, and provide a fresh perspective on your goals. I have pursued mentors in both my personal and professional lives and connected with individuals who have significantly contributed to my success.

For example, I have personally invested significant time and energy in acquiring both personal and professional mentors—people who genuinely have my best interests at heart. Mentors are often the silent force behind an individual's success. If you ask any successful person who is honest and humble, they will likely admit that their achievements were not accomplished alone.

One area where I have greatly benefited is in my spiritual life. My mentor and senior pastor, whom I've known for over a decade, has been instrumental in my spiritual growth. The support and guidance I've received from him have profoundly shaped my journey, and without our connection, the success I experience today would not have been possible.

Beyond my spiritual mentor, I have also sought out mentors in other personal and professional areas. These relationships have provided invaluable support and guidance, helping me navigate the complexities of life with greater confidence.

Benefits of Having a Mentor

- **Guidance and Advice:** Mentors provide valuable insights based on their own experiences. They can help you avoid common pitfalls and make informed decisions.

- **Skill Development:** Mentors can help you develop new skills or improve existing ones through hands-on guidance and feedback.

- **Networking Opportunities:** Mentors often have extensive networks. They can introduce you to key individuals and opportunities within your industry.

- **Confidence and Motivation:** Having someone believe in your potential can boost your confidence and motivation. Mentors provide encouragement and support during challenging times.

- **Career Advancement:** Studies show that individuals with mentors are more likely to receive promotions, raises, and career opportunities compared to those without mentors (Allen, Eby, Poteet, Lentz, & Lima, 2004).

Types of Mentors

- **Career Mentors:** Provide guidance on professional development, career advancement, and industry-specific knowledge.

- **Personal Development Mentors:** Focus on your personal growth, helping you build confidence, resilience, and self-awareness.

- **Spiritual Mentors:** Offer guidance on your spiritual journey, helping you align your actions with your beliefs and values.

Finding a Mentor

Finding the right mentor requires intentional effort. Here are some steps to help you identify and approach potential mentors:

- **Identify Your Needs:** Determine what areas you need guidance in. This could be specific skills, industry knowledge, or personal development.
- **Research Potential Mentors:** Look for individuals who have the experience and qualities you admire. This could be within your organization, industry, or network.
- **Build a Relationship:** Before formally asking someone to be your mentor, try to establish a connection. Attend events where they speak, engage with their content online, or request a casual meeting.
- **Make the Ask:** When you feel comfortable, ask them to be your mentor. Be specific about why you chose them and what you hope to gain from the relationship.
- **Set Expectations:** Discuss and agree on the frequency and mode of communication, goals, and boundaries of the mentorship.

Maintaining a Mentorship Relationship

Maintaining a productive mentorship relationship involves effort from both parties. Here are some tips to ensure a fruitful partnership:

- **Be Respectful:** Value your mentor's time and expertise. Come prepared to meetings and follow through on their advice.
- **Communicate Openly:** Share your goals, challenges, and progress honestly. Open communication fosters trust and allows your mentor to provide better guidance.
- **Show Gratitude:** Regularly express your appreciation for your mentor's support. A simple thank you can go a long way in maintaining a positive relationship.
- **Be Proactive:** Take initiative in scheduling meetings and driving the agenda. This shows your commitment and respect for the mentorship.
- **Give Back:** As you grow, find ways to give back to your mentor. This could be through introductions, sharing resources, or offering your help.

The Power of Leveraging Support Networks

A support network consists of individuals who provide emotional, professional, and sometimes financial support. This network can include family, friends, colleagues, mentors, and professional contacts. While recognizing and harnessing your potential is essential for success, leveraging your support networks can amplify your efforts and lead to even greater achievements. Success is rarely achieved alone; history shows that great men and women have tapped into their networks to accomplish extraordinary things. Building connections in both your personal and professional lives allows you to achieve more with less effort.

It's important to connect with like-minded individuals who can support you with their expertise and resources. To build a strong support network, it's crucial to surround yourself with positive influences. Be intentional about forming relationships with others who can encourage and support you in your walk with Christ (Hebrews 10:24-25). Sometimes, however, it's also beneficial to engage with people whose perspectives differ from yours. Seeking advice from those who may not agree with you can help you identify blind spots and gain new insights. For example, President Abraham Lincoln surrounded himself with people who both agreed and disagreed with him. This approach, known as his "Team of Rivals," provided diverse perspectives that strengthened his leadership during the Civil War.

When leveraging your network, focus on building genuine

connections rather than simply using people to achieve your goals. Relationships built on trust and mutual respect are more valuable and enduring. Remember, people are not tools to be used; they are valuable allies in your journey. Establishing true connections ensures that you maintain the integrity and trust needed for long-term success.

Benefits of a Strong Support Network

- **Emotional Support:** During challenging times, having a support network provides comfort, encouragement, and a sense of belonging.
- **Professional Guidance:** Your network can offer advice, feedback, and mentorship, helping you navigate your career.
- **Resources and Opportunities:** A strong support network can provide access to resources, information, and opportunities that you might not find on your own.
- **Accountability:** Your network can hold you accountable to your goals, helping you stay focused and motivated.
- **Resilience:** A robust support system enhances your resilience by providing a safety net during difficult times.

Creating a Strong Support System: Family, Friends, and Colleagues

It is a common misconception that all you need to succeed is yourself and hard work. While personal effort is undoubtedly crucial, the truth is that no one achieves success entirely on their own. If you examine the journey of anyone who has succeeded in life, you'll find they were not alone. They had people who cheered them on, supported them, and encouraged them—whether it was a parent, spouse, friend, colleague, or mentor. Every successful individual has had a network of support that played a significant role in their achievements. If you aspire to succeed in life, it is essential to build and develop networks of supporters who can guide, uplift, and help you along the way.

My own experiences have shown me the immense value of these connections. When I was working on my first book, the relationships I had cultivated with individuals in both academic and community circles were instrumental in its success. These individuals provided valuable feedback and encouragement, helping to bring my book to the general public. Their guidance, support, praise, and endorsements were crucial in making my book stand out in a vast and competitive market. While I could have attempted to do it all alone, my choice to intentionally leverage my support system made all the difference.

For instance, when I began my graduate studies at the University of Oklahoma, I already had a clear vision of what

I wanted to achieve. However, it was through a conversation with a fellow classmate, Patrick, that I learned about a case manager position opening at CREOKS. Perhaps I would have eventually discovered this opportunity on my own, but the connection with Patrick undoubtedly accelerated the process and saved me valuable time. It has been over five years since Patrick and I first met, and we have become close friends and colleagues in the field. We continue to share ideas and learn from each other. This experience, like many others, demonstrated the power of networking and the benefits of social capital. The relationships I've built with past professors, mentors, and community leaders not only provided valuable endorsements and praise for my book but also contributed to my ongoing success.

The relationships you build are invaluable and offer limitless benefits, which is why it is essential to prioritize people over material things. There is an African proverb that says, "It takes a village to raise a child." Unfortunately, in today's society, many people are isolating themselves and cutting others out of their "village." We live in a culture that often favors independence and the idea of "I, me, and myself," but the reality is that success is rarely achieved alone. If you want to succeed, you must leverage and tap into the invaluable resources that others can provide. Cherish each person within your village because there will come a time when you need them. Do not burn bridges.

Some people distance themselves from others, thinking they are better or smarter and believing they will never need anyone's help. This is a grave mistake. The truth is that every connection we make has the potential to offer support, wisdom, or opportunities that can propel us forward. It is through these connections that we can achieve our greatest successes, far beyond what we could accomplish on our own. Therefore, it is vital to cultivate and maintain these relationships, recognizing that they are a key component of any successful journey.

By prioritizing and nurturing your support networks, you not only build a strong foundation for your own success but also contribute to the success of others. This mutual exchange of support and resources creates a thriving community where everyone can achieve extraordinary outcomes.

Building and Nurturing Your Support Network

- **Identify Key People:** Determine who is already in your support network and who you need to add. This could include mentors, peers, family members, and professionals in your field.
- **Strengthen Existing Relationships:** Invest time and effort in nurturing your current relationships. Regular communication, support, and gratitude go a long way.
- **Seek New Connections:** Actively look for opportunities to meet new people who can become part of your support network. Attend events, join groups, and engage in community activities.

- **Offer Support:** Be willing to give as much as you receive. Support others in your network by offering your time, resources, and encouragement.
- **Be Consistent:** Regularly check in with your network. Consistent communication helps maintain strong and supportive relationships.

Interactive Elements

- **Networking Exercise:** List three people you admire in your field and outline a plan for reaching out to them for advice or guidance. Consider what you can offer in return to make the relationship mutually beneficial.
- **Mentorship Reflection:** Reflect on your current mentor or someone you would like to approach as a mentor. What specific guidance are you seeking? How can you show your appreciation and commitment to this relationship?
- **Support System Assessment:** Reflect on your current support network. Are there any gaps? Identify areas where you could strengthen your relationships or seek out new connections that align with your goals.

The Importance of Asking for Help

Asking for help is often seen as a sign of weakness, but in reality, it's a critical component of success. Steve Jobs once remarked that asking for help is not a sign of weakness but a predictor of success. He believed that it separates doers from dreamers. This sentiment aligns with the biblical story of Joseph, who asked Pharaoh's butler to remember him when he returned to his duties. Although the butler forgot at first, he eventually remembered Joseph at the right time, leading to Joseph's rise to power (Genesis 40:14, 23; 41:9-14).

If you find it difficult to ask for help, consider whether pride or fear of rejection might be holding you back. Rejection is a common fear, but it's important to remember that being turned down does not define you. Sometimes, people may not be able to help simply because they lack the resources or knowledge. By asking follow-up questions, you can better understand their reasons and perhaps find alternative ways to get the support you need.

Asking for help from people you know or don't know can be hard for some people, but it doesn't have to so here are some tips and strategies for effectively asking for help:

Strategies for Effectively Asking for Help:

1. Acknowledge the Need for Help

- **Self-Reflection**: Recognize when you need assistance. It's important to understand that asking for help is not a sign of weakness but a step toward growth.
- **Identify Specific Needs**: Clearly define what you need help with. Being specific about your needs makes it easier for others to offer effective assistance.

2. Choose the Right Person

- **Seek Expertise**: Approach individuals who have the knowledge or experience related to your need. This ensures that the advice or support you receive is relevant and valuable.
- **Consider Relationships**: Ask someone you trust and who understands your goals and values. A strong relationship foundation can make the conversation more comfortable.

3. Be Clear and Direct

- **Communicate Clearly**: State your request in a straightforward manner. Be clear about what you need, why you need it, and how the person can assist you.

- **Be Honest and Transparent**: Share enough context to help the person understand your situation. Transparency builds trust and encourages others to support you.

4. Be Respectful of Their Time

- **Be Considerate**: Acknowledge that the person you are asking for help may have their own commitments. Express appreciation for their time and assistance.
- **Offer Flexibility**: Suggest a time frame that works for both of you. Being flexible shows respect for the other person's schedule.

5. Show Gratitude

- **Express Appreciation**: Always thank the person for their help, regardless of the outcome. Gratitude strengthens relationships and makes people more willing to assist in the future.
- **Follow-Up**: After receiving help, follow up to share the results and how their assistance made a difference. This shows that you value their contribution.

6. Be Open to Feedback

- **Listen Actively**: When asking for help, be open to the advice and feedback you receive. Even if it's not what you expected, consider the perspective offered.
- **Implement Suggestions**: Show that you value their input by acting on the advice given. This reinforces your appreciation and encourages future support.

7. Offer Help in Return

- **Reciprocate**: If appropriate, offer your assistance in return. Building a mutual support system fosters stronger relationships.
- **Share Your Skills**: Let others know how you can be of help to them. This creates a culture of giving and receiving support.

8. Overcome the Fear of Rejection

- **Change Your Mindset**: Understand that rejection is not a reflection of your worth. People may say no for various reasons that have nothing to do with you.

- **Be Persistent**: If one person can't help, don't be discouraged. Seek assistance from others who may be in a better position to help.

9. Build a Supportive Network

- **Cultivate Relationships**: Regularly invest in building and maintaining a network of supportive individuals. Strong relationships make it easier to ask for help when needed.
- **Join Communities**: Engage in groups or communities where help is exchanged freely. This could be in professional, social, or faith-based settings.

By implementing these strategies, you can become more comfortable with asking for help, leveraging the support of others to achieve your goals, and ultimately growing both personally and professionally.

Conclusion for Step 5:

Networking, mentorship, and strong support systems are vital for success. These connections provide the guidance, opportunities, and encouragement needed to overcome challenges and achieve your goals. By actively engaging with mentors, building a diverse network, and nurturing your support system, you create a solid foundation for ongoing growth and development. Remember, success is not a solo endeavor. Embrace the power of collaboration, community, and mentorship to reach your full potential.

Next Step Reference:

The next step will focus on resilience, learning from failure, and embracing risk. These qualities are crucial for overcoming obstacles and maintaining progress, as they empower you to face challenges with confidence and determination.

| six |

Step 6: Resilience, Learning from Failure, and Embracing Risk

"THE CAVE YOU FEAR TO ENTER HOLDS THE TREASURE YOU SEEK." – JOSEPH CAMPBELL

Resilience: The Foundation of Success

Resilience is the ability to cope with tough times by drawing on inner strength and engaging support networks. It enables individuals to face difficult situations while maintaining good mental health. The American Psychological Association (APA) defines resilience as the process of adapting well in the face of adversity, trauma, tragedy, threats, or significant sources of stress. It involves the ability to maintain or regain mental health despite experiencing hardships.

Culture of Genius vs. Culture of Growth

The concept of resilience is closely related to what psychologists Murphy and Dweck (2010) describe as the "culture of genius" versus the "culture of growth." In a culture of genius, the emphasis is on innate talent and the belief that certain individuals are naturally gifted, leading to the idea that only those with such innate abilities can succeed. This environment fosters a fixed mindset, where people may avoid challenges for fear of exposing their limitations.

In contrast, a culture of growth promotes the belief that anyone can improve with effort and persistence. This environment encourages a growth mindset, where people are more likely to embrace challenges and see failures as opportunities to learn and develop. In their research, Murphy and Dweck have shown that environments characterized by a culture of growth lead to better cognitive, emotional, and behavioral outcomes because they foster a mindset that emphasizes learning and resilience.

Adopting a growth mindset involves challenging the notion that abilities are fixed and instead embracing the idea that growth is always possible. It's about having the courage to start from the beginning, to learn from mistakes, and to continually strive to improve. This mindset not only enhances personal development but also has a positive impact on how we approach challenges in all areas of life.

The Four Pillars of Resilience

Drawing from my personal experiences, including surviving multiple wars in Liberia and overcoming individual and family struggles, I have developed what I call the "Four Pillars of Resilience": Personal Values and Beliefs, Education and Knowledge, Self-awareness and Emotional Regulation, and Family and Community. These pillars form the foundation of resilience and can be cultivated to enhance one's ability to thrive in the face of adversity.

1. Personal Values and Beliefs - Embrace Healthy Thought Patterns

- Keep things in perspective: Understand that challenges are a natural part of life and can lead to growth.
- Accept change: Recognize that change is inevitable and adapt accordingly.
- Maintain a hopeful outlook: Stay optimistic about the future, even in difficult times.
- Learn from your past: Reflect on previous experiences to gain insights and strength.
- Look for opportunities for self-discovery: Use challenges as a chance to learn more about yourself and grow.

2. Education and Knowledge - Move Toward Your Goals

- Be proactive: Take initiative in pursuing your goals and seek out new opportunities.
- Help others: Engaging in acts of service can reinforce your resilience and foster a sense of community.
- Look for opportunities for self-discovery: Continually educate yourself and expand your knowledge base to better navigate challenges.

3. Self-awareness and Emotional Regulation - Foster Wellness

- Take care of your body: Physical health is closely tied to mental and emotional well-being.
- Avoid negative outlets: Steer clear of harmful behaviors or substances that can undermine your resilience.
- Practice mindfulness: Engage in practices that promote emotional regulation and mental clarity, such as meditation or deep breathing exercises.

4. Family and Community - Build Your Connections

- Develop and prioritize relationships: Strong, supportive relationships are key to resilience.
- Walk in love: Approach others with kindness and compassion, fostering a sense of belonging.
- Empathize with others: Understand and share the feelings of those around you to build stronger bonds.

- Live by the Golden Rule: Treat others as you would like to be treated, creating a positive and supportive community around you.

Learning from Failure: Turning Setbacks into Stepping Stones

Failure is an inevitable part of life, but how we respond to it determines our future success. Resilient individuals view failure not as an end but as a stepping stone toward growth. Instead of being paralyzed by setbacks, they use these experiences as opportunities to learn and improve.

Throughout my life, I have faced numerous failures and setbacks, from being rejected by a social work program to experiencing delays in my professional development. Each failure taught me valuable lessons in patience, perseverance, and trusting the process. These experiences reinforced my belief that failure is not something to be feared but embraced as a necessary part of growth.

Example of Resilience in Action

President Abraham Lincoln is one of the most profound examples of resilience in American history. Leading the nation during one of its most tumultuous periods, Lincoln demonstrated unparalleled resilience. He faced numerous personal and professional failures throughout his life, yet each setback only strengthened his resolve. Before becoming President, Lincoln faced repeated defeats in his political career, including multiple unsuccessful runs for public office.

However, these experiences did not deter him. Instead, they contributed to his development as a leader who could navigate the country through the Civil War—a time of immense uncertainty and division.

Interactive Element:

Take a moment to reflect on a recent setback in your life.

- What did you learn from the experience?

_____

- How can you apply those lessons to future challenges?

_____

- Write down your reflections and consider how they can guide you in overcoming future obstacles.

_____

Embracing Risk: The Courage to Act

Taking risks is essential for personal growth and achieving your full potential. It involves stepping outside your comfort zone, taking calculated chances, and being willing to accept the possibility of failure in pursuit of greater rewards.

President Abraham Lincoln exemplified the courage to embrace risk. His decision to issue the Emancipation Proclamation was fraught with significant personal and political risk. Yet, Lincoln recognized the moral imperative and the long-term benefits of such a bold move. By taking this calculated risk, he was able to steer the country toward a more just and unified future. Lincoln's ability to take risks was not driven by immediate outcomes but by a strong sense of purpose and a commitment to a greater cause. His leadership demonstrated that meaningful progress often requires making difficult decisions with a long-term vision in mind.

Taking risks requires the courage to face the possibility of failure. However, as Lincoln's example shows, it is through these risks that significant progress is often made. The key to embracing risk lies in being guided by your purpose and understanding that true success often comes from making bold decisions that may not yield immediate results but are aligned with your long-term goals. Fear of failure can hold you back from taking risks and seizing opportunities. It's natural to feel apprehensive about stepping into the unknown, but overcoming this fear is vital to personal and professional growth.

Think about some successful individuals like Elon Musk and J.K. Rowling, who also took significant risks in their careers. Their willingness to step into the unknown led to extraordinary success. In my journey, I've had to embrace risks, whether it was entering a field where few people who look like me succeed or challenging the institutional barriers I faced. These risks were necessary steps toward achieving my goals, and they taught me the value of resilience and determination.

The courage to take risks and try something new is what separates doers from spectators. Renowned author Brené Brown defines vulnerability as "showing up when you can't control the outcome." She emphasizes that courage is not the absence of fear but fear walking alongside you. To succeed, you must choose to venture out of your comfort zone and be vulnerable or real. Vulnerability is not a weakness, as many people think; instead, it is bravery. If it were easy, everyone would be doing it. By being one of the few who dare to do the unthinkable, you are courageous.

Angela Duckworth's concept of "grit" combines passion and perseverance as key components of long-term success. Embracing risk requires both, as it's not just about taking chances but about maintaining the determination to see them through, even when the outcome is uncertain.

Don't be afraid to fail; learn from failures and embrace risks because only those who are genuinely in the arena know what it takes to be there. As President Theodore Roosevelt eloquently stated in his famous "Man in the Arena" speech, it is not the critic who counts, but the person who is actually in the arena, striving valiantly and daring greatly.

Interactive Element:

Think about a risk you've been hesitant to take.

- What's holding you back?

_____

- What could you gain if you took the leap?

_____

- Write down your thoughts and consider taking a small step toward embracing that risk.

_____

Strategies to Embrace Risk

- **Evaluate Risks and Rewards:** Assess the potential risks and rewards of a decision or action. Consider the consequences of both success and failure and weigh them against each other.
- **Start Small:** Begin by taking small risks that stretch your comfort zone without overwhelming you. Gradually increase the level of risk as you become more comfortable with uncertainty.

- **Prepare Thoroughly:** Take the time to gather information, develop a plan, and mitigate potential risks before taking action. Preparation can increase your confidence and reduce the likelihood of failure.
- **Focus on Growth:** Shift your focus from the outcome to the process of growth and learning. Embrace challenges as opportunities to develop new skills, expand your knowledge, and build resilience.

It's important to recognize that embracing risk and learning from failure is challenging. Setbacks can be painful, and taking risks can be intimidating. However, these challenges are essential for growth. Remember, resilience is built over time, and every step you take—no matter how small—brings you closer to your goals.

Overcoming Learned Helplessness and Cultivating Hope

In the journey of personal and professional growth, one of the most significant barriers can be the sense of helplessness that develops after repeated failures or negative experiences. This phenomenon, known as learned helplessness, can prevent individuals from taking action, pursuing their goals, or even believing that change is possible.

The concept of learned helplessness was first explored by psychologist Martin Seligman. Seligman's research demonstrated that when individuals or animals are repeatedly exposed to uncontrollable negative events, they eventually stop trying to change their situation, even when opportunities for success are present. In the context of goal achievement, this can manifest as a persistent belief that one's efforts will always lead to failure, causing an individual to avoid setting new goals or pursuing new opportunities.

For individuals who have tried and failed to achieve their goals multiple times, learned helplessness can become a significant barrier to personal and professional growth. They may begin to internalize the belief that they are inherently incapable of success, leading to a cycle of inaction and continued disappointment.

Cultivating Hope as an Antidote to Learned Helplessness

To counteract learned helplessness, it is essential to cultivate hope. Hope, as defined by psychologist C.R. Snyder, involves two key components: agency (*the belief that one has the ability to achieve goals*) and pathways (*the perceived ability to generate routes to achieve those goals*). Hope is not just wishful thinking; it is an active process that empowers individuals to set and pursue goals with confidence and determination.

By fostering hope, individuals can counteract the effects of learned helplessness and build the resilience needed to navigate life's challenges. Hope motivates you to keep going, even when faced with difficulties, and helps individuals maintain a forward-looking perspective.

Practical Strategies to Cultivate Hope and Overcome Learned Helplessness:

1. **Reframe Past Failures:** Begin by reevaluating previous experiences of failure. Rather than viewing them as evidence of personal inadequacy, consider what you can learn from each setback. Understanding that failure is often a stepping stone to success can help shift your perspective and diminish the impact of learned helplessness.

2. **Set Small, Achievable Goals:** Rebuild confidence by setting small, manageable goals that are easier to

achieve. Success in these smaller tasks can create positive momentum, reinforcing the belief that you can accomplish your objectives.

3. **Develop a Growth Mindset:** Embrace the concept of a growth mindset, which is the belief that your abilities and intelligence can be developed through effort and learning. This mindset can help counteract the fixed belief that failure is inevitable and encourage you to persist in the face of difficulties.

4. **Seek Support and Feedback:** Surround yourself with supportive individuals who can offer guidance, encouragement, and constructive feedback. Having mentors or peers who believe in your potential can significantly boost your sense of agency and reinforce your pathways to success.

5. **Visualize Success:** Create a detailed mental image of achieving your goals and the steps you took to get there. Visualization can help solidify your belief in your ability to succeed and keep you motivated when challenges arise.

6. **Practice Self-Compassion:** Treat yourself with kindness and understanding, especially after setbacks. Instead of harsh self-criticism, practice self-compassion by recognizing that everyone experiences failure and that it does not define your worth or potential.

7. **Cultivate a Future-Oriented Perspective:** Focus on what you can do now to improve your future. Set new goals that excite and inspire you and remind yourself that your past does not dictate your future.

Building Mental Toughness

Building mental toughness is crucial for navigating life's challenges and setbacks. It involves developing resilience and the ability to bounce back stronger after facing adversity. Resilience is not just about bouncing back from adversity but about growing stronger through it. My book, *The Unbreakable Human Spirit of Resilience: A Boy's Journey from Adversity to Triumph*, showcases resilience in action. From the slums of West Point and the war-torn streets of Liberia, where I was minutes away from being killed by a rocket, to becoming a mental health counselor in the United States, this journey exemplifies how resilience can help us overcome even the most daunting challenges. In my role today, I continue to fulfill my purpose and give back to my community, embodying the resilient spirit that has shaped my life.

In the book of Romans 5:3-5, the Apostle Paul highlights the transformative power of resilience, stating, "We also glory in our sufferings, because we know that suffering produces perseverance; perseverance, character; and character, hope." This passage underscores the idea that the trials we endure build our resilience, shaping our character and giving rise to hope.

Conclusion for Step 6: Building Your Resilience

Integrating the concepts of resilience, learned helplessness, hope, and risk-taking into your mindset and daily practices will empower you to move beyond the limitations imposed by past experiences. By cultivating hope, leveraging the support of others, embracing risks, and taking practical steps to build resilience, you can achieve your full potential and thrive in the face of adversity. This approach ensures that, no matter how many times you've encountered setbacks, you remain committed to your goals and continue to pursue them with renewed energy and determination.

The lives of Abraham Lincoln, Elon Musk, and J.K. Rowling offer powerful insights into the nature of resilience and the courage to embrace risk. Lincoln's ability to overcome repeated failures, Musk's visionary persistence in the face of monumental challenges, and Rowling's unwavering belief in her story despite numerous rejections exemplify the qualities necessary to achieve extraordinary success. Their journeys demonstrate that resilience is not about avoiding difficulties but about confronting them head-on, learning from each setback, and transforming adversity into opportunities for growth.

In your own journey, consider how you can build resilience by embracing your challenges, learning from your failures, and taking bold actions aligned with your purpose. Like Lincoln, Musk, and Rowling, you have the capacity to develop the strength to persevere through hardships and the wisdom to guide others during trying times.

Resilience, combined with a willingness to embrace risk, is key to unlocking your extraordinary potential and achieving the impossible. By adopting this mindset, you equip yourself to navigate life's uncertainties with confidence, determination, and a deep sense of purpose, paving the way for remarkable achievements. Whether in personal endeavors or professional aspirations, the courage to take risks and the resilience to endure setbacks will set you apart as someone who is not just surviving but thriving in the face of adversity.

Next Step Reference:

In the final step, we will discuss the importance of character development, celebrating milestones, sustaining progress, and giving back to your community. These actions not only reinforce your achievements but also inspire continuous growth and fulfillment.

Activities and Assessments

Building Mental Toughness

Activity 1: Reflecting on Past Setbacks

Instructions: Identify a Past Setback: Think about a significant setback or failure you experienced in the past

Reflect: Answer the following questions in a journal:

- What was the setback?
- How did it make you feel at the time?
- What actions did you take in response to the setback?
- What did you learn from this experience?
- How has this setback shaped your current perspective and actions?

Assessment:

1. Reflect on your answers and identify patterns or themes. Consider how you can apply the lessons learned to future challenges. This reflection will help you recognize your ability to overcome adversity and build confidence in your resilience.
2. Monitor your self-talk and notice any changes in

your attitude toward challenges and failures. Track your progress by noting any shifts in your mindset and resilience over time.

Activity 3: Building a Resilience Toolkit

Instructions:

Identify Coping Strategies: List the strategies that help you cope with stress and setbacks. These might include exercise, meditation, talking to a friend, or engaging in hobbies.

Create a Toolkit: Assemble physical or digital resources related to your coping strategies, such as guided meditation apps, exercise plans, or contact information for supportive friends or mentors.

Plan for Setbacks: Develop a plan for how you will use your resilience toolkit when faced with future setbacks. Include specific actions and resources you will turn to for support.

Assessment:

Evaluate the effectiveness of your resilience toolkit by using it during a challenging situation. Reflect on how well the strategies worked and make any necessary adjustments to improve your toolkit.

Embracing Risk

Activity 4: Risk Assessment and Management

Instructions:

Identify a Risk: Think about a risk you have been hesitant to take, whether in your personal or professional life.

Analyze the Risk: Answer the following questions:

- What are the potential benefits of taking this risk?
- What are the potential downsides or consequences?
- What can you do to mitigate these downsides?

Create an Action Plan: Develop a step-by-step plan for taking the risk, including any precautions or preparations you need to make.

Assessment: After taking the risk, evaluate the outcome and reflect on the experience. What did you learn? How did taking the risk impact your confidence and growth? Use this reflection to inform future risk-taking decisions.

Activity 5: Risk-Taking Challenge

Instructions:

Set a Goal: Choose a specific, meaningful goal that involves taking a calculated risk. This could be starting a new project, pursuing a new career opportunity, or learning a new skill.

Break It Down: Divide the goal into smaller, manageable steps. Identify the risks associated with each step and plan how you will address them.

Take Action: Begin taking the steps toward your goal, one at a time. Keep a journal to document your progress, challenges, and reflections.

Assessment:

Review your journal entries regularly to track your progress and identify any patterns in your risk-taking behavior. Reflect on how embracing risk has contributed to your personal and professional growth.

| seven |

Step 7: Character Development, Celebrating Milestones, and Sustaining Progress

"SUCCESS IS NOT FINAL, FAILURE IS NOT FATAL: IT IS THE COURAGE TO CONTINUE THAT COUNTS." - WINSTON CHURCHILL

As you reach the final step of this journey, it's important to recognize that true success is not just about achieving your goals—it's about sustaining that success and continuing to grow. Step 7 focuses on the essential components that will help you not only celebrate the milestones you've reached but also maintain the momentum needed for ongoing progress.

Character development is at the heart of lasting success.

The traits you've cultivated throughout this journey—resilience, adaptability, humility, integrity, perseverance, self-discipline, and trust—are more than just qualities; they are the foundation that will support you through life's challenges and triumphs. While your talents and gifts may open doors, it is your character that will keep you there, guiding you to make decisions that align with your values and helping you overcome obstacles with grace and determination.

In this step, we'll explore how to integrate these character traits into your daily life, celebrate your achievements in a meaningful way, and sustain your progress through continuous development and service to others. By embracing the lessons learned and the growth experienced, you will be better equipped to achieve the impossible and leave a lasting impact on the world around you.

Character Development: The Foundation of Lasting Success

Character development is not merely a step toward achieving your goals; it is the foundation upon which long-term success is built. The qualities you cultivate—resilience, adaptability, humility, integrity, perseverance, self-discipline, and trust—are the traits that will carry you through life's inevitable challenges and triumphs. The saying "Your talents and gifts will take you places, but your character will keep you there" captures this truth. This is not just motivational rhetoric; it is a fundamental reality for anyone striving to achieve the extraordinary.

The previous six steps of your journey were about recognizing and harnessing your extraordinary potential. While these steps are essential for challenging the status quo and achieving the impossible, they are only part of the equation. Think of these steps as the finest ingredients needed to bake a cake. However, without the crucial process of baking—representing character development—the cake will remain unfinished and inedible. No matter how beautiful the cake may appear, if it isn't fully baked, it will not serve its purpose, and all your efforts will ultimately go to waste.

For those who achieve success ethically, character development is the process that sustains true success. Some may reach the top through unethical means—by lying, cheating, belittling, or stepping on others—but such success is fleeting. Without integrity and trust, success will eventually crumble, as light and darkness cannot coexist. The process of "baking the cake" represents character development, and it is this process that sustains true success. It's the part of the journey that many resist, yet it is essential. While everyone dreams of standing on the summit of Mount Everest, few are willing to endure the rigorous climb it demands.

The path to the peak is not a smooth ride filled with accolades. Instead, it requires self-discipline, humility, integrity, and patience. There will be dark, cold nights, moments of doubt, and times when you may be overlooked or mistreated. However, just as muscles grow stronger after being torn down during a workout, these challenges build and develop your character. What may seem difficult becomes manageable once you are clear about your goals and committed to your journey.

Engaging in character development is the key to achieving what might seem impossible. It is the one factor that will sustain you through tough times because once you've cultivated these traits, no challenge will be too great for you to overcome. As President Franklin D. Roosevelt wisely said, "It's not the critic who counts." What truly matters is the courage to persevere, the integrity to uphold your values, and the character to sustain your success.

Let's explore how each of these character traits plays a crucial role in sustaining progress and ensuring continued success.

Adaptability: Thriving in a Rapidly Changing World

Understanding Adaptability: A Key to Success

In an era of constant change, adaptability has become an essential skill for both personal and professional success. Adaptability is essential for both personal and professional success in an era of constant change. It involves the ability to adjust strategies, behaviors, emotions, and thoughts to cope with new, changing, or unexpected situations effectively. Adaptability ensures that you remain flexible while staying committed to your goals, allowing you to embrace new opportunities and overcome obstacles. It is a critical skill in managing uncertainty and complexity in various contexts.

Adaptability is closely linked with resilience, a trait that enables individuals to recover from setbacks and continue moving forward. Together, these qualities form the backbone of success in a dynamic world.

Strategies to Build Adaptability

1. Cultivate a Growth Mindset and Curiosity:

- A growth mindset, as outlined by psychologist Carol Dweck, is the belief that abilities and intelligence can be developed through effort and learning. This mindset is essential for adaptability because it fosters curiosity and a willingness to explore new ideas and perspectives. Leaders should create environments that encourage continuous learning and view failures as opportunities for growth.
- *Biblical Insight*: Proverbs 1:5 says, "Let the wise hear and increase in learning, and the one who understands obtain guidance." This emphasizes the importance of a mindset open to learning and growth.

2. Encourage Risk-Taking:

- Building a culture of adaptability requires encouraging risk-taking and experimentation. Organizations that reward innovation and allow for failure create a safe space for employees to try new approaches without fear of repercussions. This promotes innovation and builds resilience as employees learn to adapt to both successes and setbacks.

- *Activity*: Reflect on a recent decision where you played it safe. What would have happened if you had taken a calculated risk? How might that have led to growth?

3. Prioritize Effective Communication:

- Communication is a cornerstone of adaptability. Ensuring that all team members are kept informed and aligned allows for quicker and more effective responses to change. Regular updates and transparent discussions help teams stay on the same page and reduce confusion during transitions.
- *Strategy*: Implement regular team check-ins to discuss ongoing projects and potential changes. Encourage open dialogue about challenges and opportunities.

4. Create a Safe Environment for Experimentation:

- To cultivate adaptability, it's important to create an environment where employees feel safe to experiment and innovate. Recognizing and rewarding effort, even if it leads to failure, encourages a culture of continuous improvement. This fosters the development of critical thinking and creativity—skills that are essential for adapting to change.

- *Assessment*: Evaluate your workplace environment. Does it encourage experimentation, or are employees hesitant to try new things? What can be done to create a more supportive environment for innovation?

5. Invest in Employee Training and Development:

- Ongoing training and development are critical for maintaining adaptability in the workforce. Providing employees with the necessary skills and knowledge ensures they are well-equipped to handle new challenges as they arise. This investment in employee growth enhances adaptability and keeps the workforce engaged and motivated.
- *Strategy*: Offer regular workshops and courses that focus on emerging industry trends and skills. Encourage employees to pursue personal development that aligns with their career goals.

6. Embrace Discomfort and Challenge:

- Making discomfort a routine part of the work culture can significantly enhance adaptability. When employees regularly face and overcome challenges, they become more resilient and better prepared for future changes. Leaders can facilitate this growth by introducing challenges that push employees out of their comfort zones.

- *Biblical Insight:* James 1:2-4 teaches, "Consider it pure joy, my brothers and sisters, whenever you face trials of many kinds, because you know that the testing of your faith produces perseverance." Embracing challenges strengthens character and builds resilience.

7. Focus on the Future:

- A forward-looking approach is crucial for building adaptability. By staying informed about industry trends and potential disruptions, organizations can anticipate changes and prepare accordingly. This proactive mindset allows teams to stay ahead of the curve and adapt more quickly to new developments.
- *Strategy:* Implement regular strategy sessions to review market trends and predict potential changes. Encourage teams to brainstorm how these trends could impact their work and plan accordingly.

The Impact of Adaptability on Well-Being and Relationships

Adaptability plays a crucial role in well-being and interpersonal relationships. Research shows that adaptability can reduce burnout by promoting a flexible approach to challenges and helping individuals maintain a healthy work-life balance. Employees who feel supported in adapting to change experience higher levels of engagement and job satisfaction.

Moreover, adaptability enhances interpersonal relationships by fostering empathy and vulnerability. In today's increasingly virtual work environments, adaptability is key to maintaining strong relationships and effective communication.

Adaptability Across Organizational Levels

Adaptability operates at various levels within an organization:

1. **Individual**: At the individual level, adaptability improves well-being by enabling employees to manage stress and change effectively. It promotes resilience, helping individuals cope with the pressures of a rapidly changing environment.
2. **Interpersonal**: Adaptability enhances the ability to build and maintain strong relationships. By being open to change and empathetic towards others, individuals can create more meaningful connections and foster a positive work environment.
3. **Team**: At the team level, adaptability strengthens collaboration and psychological safety. Teams that trust and care for each other are better equipped to handle stress and adapt to new challenges, leading to higher levels of engagement and performance.

4. **Organizational**: Organizational adaptability creates a culture that supports innovation, agility, and resilience. By embedding adaptability into the organization's foundation, companies can thrive in ambiguity and uncertainty, ensuring long-term success.

The Strategic Advantage of Adaptability

Adaptability is a vital skill that enables individuals and organizations to navigate change, embrace new opportunities, and continue growing. By cultivating a culture of adaptability, organizations can enhance well-being, strengthen relationships, and drive innovation. Leaders play a crucial role in modeling adaptability, fostering a growth mindset, and providing the support needed to thrive in a constantly changing environment. As Proverbs 19:20 advises, "Listen to advice and accept discipline, and at the end, you will be counted among the wise." Embracing adaptability as a core value allows individuals and organizations to turn challenges into opportunities, ensuring long-term resilience and growth.

Humility and Growth: Embracing a Learning Mindset

Humility is a cornerstone of personal and professional growth. Humility is the ability to maintain a balanced view of oneself, acknowledging personal strengths and limitations without an inflated sense of self-importance. Current research underscores the critical role humility plays in development, enabling individuals to find value in opportunities even when circumstances do not align with their expectations. It includes openness to new ideas, feedback, and the recognition of others' contributions.

In the context of servant leadership, humility is defined as an awareness of one's strengths and weaknesses, the capacity to keep accomplishments and talents in perspective, and a willingness to admit fallibility and mistakes. Humble individuals are more likely to view smaller opportunities as essential stepping stones toward larger goals, while those driven by pride or arrogance may dismiss these chances, ultimately hindering their progress.

Humility as a Way of Life

Humility is more than just a trait; it's a way of life that enriches every aspect of your journey. It opens the door to continuous learning, strengthens relationships, and amplifies your impact as both a leader and an individual.

Humility enables you to recognize the value others bring

to your journey, making it easier to seek advice, mentorship, and support when needed. A humble mindset allows you to embrace opportunities such as serving others, cleaning, or volunteering in your local civic or religious organization, viewing them as small but meaningful steps toward greater accomplishments. In contrast, pride and arrogance may lead you to dismiss these opportunities as beneath you, potentially missing out on experiences that could propel you forward. By cultivating humility, you unlock a deeper sense of purpose and forge a stronger connection with the world around you, paving the way for lasting success.

Characteristics of Humility

Self-Awareness:

Humility begins with self-awareness. It involves recognizing your strengths and weaknesses without inflating or diminishing your value. Self-aware individuals are honest about their abilities and limitations, which allows them to seek help when needed and continue their personal development.

Openness to Feedback:

Humble people actively seek feedback and are open to criticism. They understand that constructive feedback is essential for growth and use it to improve their performance and relationships.

Gratitude:

Gratitude is a crucial component of humility. It involves acknowledging the contributions of others to your success and expressing appreciation for their efforts. Humble individuals recognize that they didn't achieve success alone and are thankful for the support and opportunities they've received.

Empathy:

Humility and empathy go hand in hand. Humble individuals are attuned to the feelings and needs of others. They listen actively, offer support, and show genuine concern for the well-being of those around them.

Modesty:

Modesty is the outward expression of humility. It's the ability to achieve success without seeking excessive praise or attention. Humble people let their actions speak for themselves and share credit with others.

Willingness to Learn:

Humble individuals are lifelong learners. They understand that they don't have all the answers and are eager to learn from others, regardless of their status or experience.

Respect for Others:

Humility fosters respect for others. Humble leaders and individuals treat everyone with dignity, regardless of their position or background. They value diverse perspectives and create environments where everyone feels valued.

Humility in Personal and Professional Growth

Humility is often misunderstood as a sign of weakness, but it is one of the most powerful traits a person can cultivate. It allows you to learn from others, acknowledge your mistakes, and remain grounded, no matter how successful you become. In both leadership and interpersonal relationships, humility is transformative. It's a trait that not only enhances your character but also amplifies your influence on those around you. Humble leaders inspire trust, foster collaboration, and create a positive organizational culture. They lead by example, demonstrating that true leadership is about serving others and working toward a collective goal.

To recognize the extraordinary within yourself, humility is essential. It enables you to acknowledge your achievements while understanding the importance of continuous learning and growth. Humility also allows you to recognize when you need help and reach out for support. A mindset that says, "I'm enough, I know it all," or "Who is this person to tell me what to do? I have more experience and degrees," stems from pride and ego—barriers that can prevent you from achieving the extraordinary.

Once you become aware that your ego may be the one thing standing between you and your full potential, you can take steps to overcome it. Humility allows you to be open to learning from anyone, even a child. As Jesus illustrated when He said, "Therefore, whoever humbles himself like this child is the greatest in the kingdom of heaven" (Matthew 18:4), greatness is not about status or superiority but about the willingness to be humble and serve.

The Humble Leader's Impact

Building Trust:

Humble leaders build trust by being transparent, honest, and approachable. They admit their mistakes and take responsibility for their actions, encouraging others to do the same.

Encouraging Collaboration:

Humble leaders understand that great ideas can come from anyone, and they encourage collaboration by creating an inclusive environment. They empower their teams to contribute their ideas and expertise, leading to more innovative and effective solutions.

Promoting Growth:

By being open to feedback and learning, humble leaders promote a culture of growth and continuous improvement. They provide opportunities for their team members to develop their skills and advance in their careers.

Creating a Positive Work Environment:

Humble leaders treat their employees with respect and empathy, creating a positive work environment. They recognize and celebrate the contributions of others, boosting morale and motivation.

Serving Others:

At the core of humble leadership is the desire to serve others. Humble leaders prioritize the needs of their team and work towards creating value for their organization and its stakeholders.

Humility in Interpersonal Relationships

Humility is equally vital in interpersonal relationships. Whether in friendships, family, or romantic relationships, humility fosters deeper connections and mutual respect.

The Role of Humility in Relationships

Active Listening:

Humility enables you to listen actively to others, valuing their perspectives and feelings. This deepens understanding and strengthens the bond between individuals.

Resolving Conflicts:

Humble individuals approach conflicts with a willingness to compromise and find common ground. They prioritize the relationship over being right, leading to more harmonious interactions.

Mutual Respect:

Humility fosters mutual respect by acknowledging the strengths and contributions of others. In relationships, this creates a sense of equality and partnership.

Apologizing and Forgiving:

Humility allows individuals to apologize sincerely when they've made a mistake and to forgive others when they've been wronged. This helps to heal wounds and maintain healthy relationships.

Supporting Others:

Humble individuals are supportive of others' successes and challenges. They offer help without expecting anything in return, which strengthens the relationship.

Humility in Practice: Time Management, Prioritization, and Continuous Learning

In the context of time management, prioritization, and continuous learning, humility plays a crucial role. It helps you recognize that there is always more to learn and that others, regardless of their status or experience, may have valuable insights. By being humble, you remain open to growth, which is essential for achieving long-term success. Humility also helps you prioritize your goals and manage your time more effectively, as it keeps you grounded and focused on what truly matters.

Cultivating humility is not just about being modest; it's about fostering an attitude that opens doors to learning, growth, and extraordinary achievements. Recognizing the role of humility in your journey can help you overcome obstacles, build stronger relationships, and ultimately achieve the impossible.

Activities to Cultivate Humility

Activity 1: The Humility Journal
Purpose: *To develop self-awareness and gratitude by reflecting on daily experiences.*

Instructions:

- **Daily Reflection**: Each day, write down three things you are grateful for. These can include personal achievements, support from others, or simple pleasures.
- **Identify Lessons**: Reflect on a situation where you had to admit a mistake or where you learned something new from someone else. Write down the lesson you learned and how it impacted you.
- **Acknowledge Others**: Write about someone who made a positive impact on your life that day and consider how you can express your appreciation to them.

Solution:

- **Example Entry**: "Today, I'm grateful for the support of my team in completing the project. I learned the importance of clear communication when I realized a mistake in the project plan. I appreciate my colleague pointing it out and helping me correct it."

Activity 2: Seeking Feedback
Purpose: *To foster growth and continuous improvement by actively seeking feedback.*

Instructions:

- **Identify Areas for Improvement**: Choose one area in your personal or professional life where you'd like to improve.
- **Seek Feedback**: Ask a trusted friend, colleague, or mentor for honest feedback on how you can improve in that area.
- **Implement Changes**: Reflect on the feedback and create a plan to implement the suggested changes.
- **Follow-Up**: After a few weeks, ask for feedback again to assess your progress.

Solution:

- **Example**: "I asked my supervisor for feedback on my time management skills. She suggested prioritizing tasks more effectively by using a project management tool. I've started using the tool and have seen a significant improvement in meeting deadlines."

Integrity: The Cornerstone of Character and Leadership

Integrity is the alignment between one's values, principles, and actions. It involves staying true to these principles, even when facing challenges or temptations. Integrity is not just about being honest in the moment but about consistently applying ethical principles across all areas of life. It's what ensures that success is achieved through ethical means and that the journey to success is as honorable as the destination.

Research by Peterson and Seligman (2004) categorizes integrity as a key character strength, encompassing honesty, morality, and trustworthiness. These traits are crucial for both personal development and effective leadership, fostering trust, reliability, and respect in relationships and organizations.

Building and Demonstrating Integrity as a Leader

1. Model Integrity Consistently: Leaders must set an example by consistently displaying integrity. This means being honest, owning up to mistakes, giving credit where it is due, and treating everyone with respect. As Moe Rock, CEO of the Los Angeles Tribune, emphasizes, a leader's actions speak louder than words, and by modeling integrity, they set a standard for others to follow. This approach creates a culture of trust and ethical behavior within the organization.

- **Strategy to Build Integrity**: Regularly reflect on your decisions and actions, ensuring they align with your core values. Surround yourself with individuals who hold you accountable and challenge you to maintain high ethical standards. James 4:17 reminds us, "If anyone, then, knows the good they ought to do and doesn't do it, it is sin for them." This calls for active integrity in decision-making and leadership. Research by Mayer, Davis, and Schoorman (1995) highlights that leaders who consistently model integrity are more likely to inspire trust and commitment within their teams.

2. Fulfill Promises and Keep Commitments: Integrity involves keeping promises and honoring commitments. This principle applies to both professional responsibilities and personal obligations. Research suggests that fulfilling commitments enhances trust and strengthens relationships, which is critical for sustained success (Simons, 2002).

- **Strategy to Build Integrity**: Before making any commitments, carefully evaluate whether you can deliver on them. Proverbs 20:25 warns, "It is a trap to dedicate something rashly and only later to consider one's vows." This highlights the importance of thoughtful commitment-making in maintaining integrity.

3. Thoughtful Commitment-Making: Before making any commitments, evaluate whether you can deliver on them. Learning to say no when necessary is crucial to maintaining integrity, as overcommitting can lead to broken promises and damaged trust. A study by Lewicki, McAllister, and Bies (1998) indicates that thoughtful commitment-making is essential for maintaining trust in both personal and professional relationships.

4. Foster a Culture of Accountability: Create an environment where everyone is held accountable for their actions. Establish clear expectations, provide regular feedback, and implement systems that encourage accountability. According to research by Colquitt, Conlon, Wesson, Porter, and Ng (2001), a culture of accountability is linked to higher levels of trust and organizational performance.

- **Strategy to Build Integrity**: Encourage open communication and regular self-assessment within your team. Colossians 3:23-24 advises, "Whatever you do, work at it with all your heart, as working for the Lord, not for human masters, since you know that you will receive an inheritance from the Lord as a reward." This perspective encourages accountability as a form of integrity in work and service.

5. Prioritize Open Communication: Integrity thrives in environments where communication is open and transparent. Encourage your team or peers to voice concerns and ideas without fear of retaliation. Research shows that open communication is a key component of ethical climates in organizations and is strongly associated with organizational trust and integrity (Bies & Tripp, 1996).

6. Integrate Ethical Decision-Making: Incorporate ethical considerations into your decision-making processes. This involves looking beyond what is most profitable or convenient and considering what is right and fair. Research by Treviño, Brown, and Hartman (2003) emphasizes the importance of ethical decision-making in maintaining integrity and fostering a culture of ethics within organizations.

- **Strategy to Build Integrity**: Establish a clear code of ethics and ensure it is communicated and upheld throughout your organization. Micah 6:8 emphasizes, "He has shown you, O mortal, what is good. And what does the Lord require of you? To act justly and to love mercy and to walk humbly with your God." This verse serves as a foundation for ethical decision-making rooted in integrity.

7. **Reflect and Improve**: Regular self-reflection is key to building and maintaining integrity. Examine your decisions and actions to ensure they align with your core values, and identify areas for improvement. Research suggests that self-reflection and ethical self-awareness are critical for sustaining integrity and enhancing leadership effectiveness (Brown & Treviño, 2006).

Application and Activities

- **Self-Assessment**: Regularly evaluate your actions and decisions against your core values. Ask yourself if you are consistently acting with integrity in both personal and professional settings.
- **Open Communication Exercise**: Encourage a culture of transparency by holding regular meetings where team members can voice their concerns and ideas without fear of retaliation.
- **Ethical Dilemma Scenarios**: Engage in exercises where you must make decisions based on ethical considerations, discussing the outcomes and reflecting on how they align with your values.

Integrating Character Development with Milestones

Every milestone is a reflection of your character, and each celebration is an opportunity to reinforce the traits that have gotten you this far. Regular self-reflection and continuous improvement in integrity-related behaviors are essential for both personal and organizational growth. By doing so, you ensure that your progress is not just a series of isolated victories but part of a broader journey of personal and professional growth.

Reflective Question:

- How can you use the character traits you've developed —such as integrity, perseverance, self-discipline, and adaptability—to sustain your progress and continue achieving your goals?
- In what ways can celebrating your milestones reinforce your commitment to your core values and long-term vision?

Perseverance: The Path to Success and Growth

Understanding Perseverance: The Engine of Success

Perseverance is the sustained effort that enables individuals to overcome obstacles and achieve long-term goals. It's the ability to keep striving toward an objective despite difficulties, delays, or failures. Celebrating milestones along your journey acknowledges your achievements and serves as a reminder of the perseverance required to reach each one.

Perseverance and patience are distinct yet complementary traits. Perseverance involves actively pursuing goals with determination, while patience allows you to endure delays and challenges without becoming frustrated. Together, they form a powerful combination that supports long-term success, prevents burnout, and encourages thoughtful progress.

Strategies to Build Perseverance

1. **Set Small, Achievable Goals**: Break down large objectives into smaller, manageable tasks. Celebrating small wins helps maintain momentum and reinforces the belief that progress, no matter how incremental, leads to significant outcomes. This aligns with the concept of incremental progress, which builds confidence and perseverance over time.

2. **Recall Past Perseverance**: Reflect on past experiences where you persisted through challenges. Recalling these

moments can strengthen your resolve and remind you of your ability to overcome obstacles.

3. **Take Small Steps**: When faced with a daunting goal, identify one small action you can take immediately. This reduces overwhelm and allows for incremental progress, leading to larger accomplishments over time.

4. **Set a Reasonable Pace**: Avoid frenzied activity or burnout by pacing yourself. Perseverance is essential for long-term goals, making it important to maintain a steady, sustainable pace. As the saying goes, "Slow and steady wins the race."

5. **Try Alternative Solutions**: If you find yourself stuck, explore different ways to achieve your goal. Flexibility in your approach can prevent stagnation and encourage continuous progress.

6. **Be Patient and Give Things Time**: Recognize that significant achievements often take time. Patience is essential in allowing your efforts to bear fruit, especially when progress seems slow or stalled.

7. **Adapt and Learn from Mistakes**: View challenges and setbacks as learning opportunities. Analyze what went wrong, adjust your approach, and use these lessons to improve your chances of success in the future. Proverbs 24:16 reminds us, "For though the righteous fall seven times, they rise again," emphasizing the importance of resilience and learning from setbacks.

8. **Stay Aligned with Your Values and Interests**: Perseverance is most sustainable when it aligns with your core values and passions. Regularly remind yourself of

why your goals are important, and stay connected to the motivations that drive your efforts. Galatians 6:9 encourages us, "Let us not become weary in doing good, for at the proper time we will reap a harvest if we do not give up," reinforcing the importance of perseverance in alignment with our values.

The Role of Perseverance in Character Development

Perseverance is not just a trait for achieving success; it is also crucial for character development. Carol Dweck's research on mindset as discussed in Step 1 highlights that perseverance contributes to a growth mindset. Individuals with a growth mindset are more likely to persevere through challenges and achieve greater success. Perseverance also plays a key role in resilience, as it enables individuals to continue pushing forward despite setbacks, forming a strong foundation for navigating life's challenges. Perseverance is not just about reaching a destination; it's about the journey of continuous growth, learning, and improvement. By building perseverance, you enhance your ability to overcome obstacles and achieve your objectives, ultimately leading to greater success and fulfillment.

Research has consistently shown that perseverance is a key predictor of success. Duckworth's studies reveal that individuals with high levels of perseverance are more likely to achieve their goals, regardless of their natural abilities. Additionally, perseverance is linked to self-regulation—the ability to control one's emotions, thoughts, and behaviors in pursuit of long-term goals. Research published in the *Journal of Personality and Social Psychology* indicates that combining self-regulation with perseverance significantly enhances the likelihood of success.

Scripture also emphasizes the importance of perseverance. James 1:12 states, "Blessed is the one who perseveres under trial because, having stood the test, that person will receive the crown of life that the Lord has promised to those who love him." This verse highlights the spiritual rewards of perseverance and encourages believers to endure challenges with faith and determination.

Perseverance is a crucial trait that underpins success, resilience, and personal growth. It involves sustained effort, even in the face of challenges, and is closely related to patience, which allows for the strategic pacing of that effort. Together, these traits enable individuals to pursue long-term goals with determination and resilience, leading to greater success and fulfillment.

By implementing practical strategies for building perseverance, such as setting small goals, reflecting on past successes, and maintaining alignment with core values, individuals can enhance their ability to overcome obstacles and achieve their objectives. Ultimately, perseverance is not just about reaching a destination; it's about the journey of continuous growth, learning, and improvement.

Reflective Activity:

- **Perseverance Journal**: Begin a journal dedicated to tracking your perseverance journey. Each day, note any challenges you faced and how you responded. Reflect on what helped you push through and what you might do differently next time. Over time, this journal will serve as a powerful reminder of your growth and the progress you've made.
- **Perseverance Assessment**: Periodically assess your perseverance by reflecting on how you handle setbacks. Ask yourself: Do I give up easily when faced with challenges, or do I look for alternative solutions? How can I strengthen my perseverance? Use these reflections to identify areas for improvement and to celebrate your successes in maintaining perseverance.

Incorporating these practices into your daily routine will not only help you develop perseverance but also reinforce the other character traits essential to sustaining progress and achieving long-term success.

The Role of Discipline in Achieving Long-Term Success

Understanding Self-Discipline: The Backbone of Achievement

Self-discipline refers to the ability to control one's emotions, thoughts, and behaviors in the face of temptations and impulses. It involves maintaining focus on long-term goals, resisting short-term gratifications, and effectively managing time. Self-discipline is the driving force behind consistent progress toward long-term objectives. As you celebrate milestones, it's essential to reflect on the pivotal role self-discipline has played in your achievements and to reaffirm your commitment to maintaining it as you pursue future goals.

The Strategic Importance of Discipline

Discipline is not just a habit; it is a strategic tool that enables individuals to achieve their long-term goals. By cultivating self-discipline, you can remain focused on your objectives, resist short-term temptations, and make steady progress even in the face of challenges. Celebrating milestones provides an opportunity to acknowledge the role discipline has played in your journey and to recommit to its importance as you move forward.

In psychological research, self-discipline is often explored through the concept of "ego depletion," which suggests that willpower is a finite resource that can be depleted with use. Baumeister et al.'s (1998) "cookie experiment" illustrated that exerting self-control in one area could reduce one's ability to exercise self-discipline in subsequent tasks. However, subsequent research, such as that by Job et al. (2013), has shown that beliefs about willpower can significantly impact self-discipline. Those who view willpower as an unlimited resource are often better able to maintain self-control even after facing challenges.

Moreover, the famous marshmallow experiment by Mischel and Ebbesen (1970) demonstrated that children who could delay gratification were more likely to experience better academic and social outcomes later in life. This underscores the long-term benefits of self-discipline in various areas, including academic performance, health, and career success.

Strategies for Building and Maintaining Self-Discipline

1. Create a Routine Aligned with Your Goals: Establishing a daily routine that aligns with your long-term goals is one of the most effective ways to build self-discipline. By structuring your day around consistent habits, you reduce decision fatigue and make it easier to stay on track. For instance, dedicating specific times to work, exercise, and personal development helps you maintain focus and avoid distractions.

- *Biblical Insight*: Proverbs 16:3 advises, "Commit to the Lord whatever you do, and he will establish your plans." This emphasizes the importance of discipline and commitment in achieving success.

2. Practice Delaying Gratification: Delaying gratification involves resisting the temptation of immediate rewards in favor of long-term benefits. This skill is crucial for self-discipline. Regularly practicing delayed gratification, such as choosing to work on important tasks instead of indulging in leisure activities, strengthens your willpower and enhances your ability to stay committed to your goals.

- *Activity*: Identify one area where you can practice delaying gratification this week. Reflect on the long-term benefits of this choice and how it aligns with your goals.

3. Develop Self-Awareness: Increasing self-awareness helps you identify situations where you are most likely to face temptations or distractions. By understanding these triggers, you can develop strategies to manage them effectively. For example, if you know that you are more likely to make impulsive decisions when tired, you can plan to tackle important tasks earlier in the day.

- *Strategy*: Keep a journal for a week, noting when you feel most tempted to stray from your goals. Reflect on ways to address these triggers proactively.

4. Believe in the Power of Willpower: Adopting a mindset that views self-discipline as an unlimited resource can empower you to push through challenges without feeling depleted. By shifting your beliefs about willpower, you can enhance your capacity to maintain self-control even after facing significant effort earlier in the day.

- *Biblical Insight*: Philippians 4:13 reminds us, "I can do all things through Christ who strengthens me." This scripture reinforces the idea that with the right mindset and faith, we have the strength to persevere.

5. Engage in Regular Physical Exercise: Physical exercise is not only good for your body but also enhances self-discipline by improving overall self-regulation. Regular exercise requires willpower, and this practice can spill over into other areas of life, improving your ability to control impulses and stay focused on your goals.

- *Activity*: Set a goal to incorporate at least 30 minutes of physical activity into your daily routine. Reflect on how this commitment strengthens your discipline in other areas.

6. Use Implementation Intentions: Implementation intentions involve creating specific "if-then" plans that outline how you will respond to particular challenges or temptations. For example, "If I feel the urge to procrastinate, then I will spend five minutes reviewing my to-do list." This technique bridges the gap between intentions and actions, making it easier to follow through on your goals.

- *Assessment*: Identify a recurring challenge you face and create an implementation intention to address it. Track your success over the next week.

The Impact of Self-Discipline on Long-Term Success

Research consistently shows that self-discipline is a critical factor in achieving long-term success across various domains. For instance, studies have found that self-discipline is a stronger predictor of academic success than intelligence. Students with higher levels of self-discipline tend to have better grades, higher attendance rates, and superior test scores.

In addition to academic and career success, self-discipline is also linked to better health outcomes. Individuals with higher self-discipline are more likely to maintain healthy habits, such as regular exercise and a balanced diet, and are less likely to engage in risky behaviors. This leads to a lower risk of obesity, better physical fitness, and overall improved well-being.

Discipline is not just about adhering to rules or routines; it is a strategic tool that enables individuals to achieve their long-term goals. By cultivating self-discipline, you can stay focused on your objectives, resist short-term temptations, and make consistent progress even in the face of challenges.

As you celebrate milestones, it's important to recognize the role that discipline has played in your achievements and to commit to maintaining this discipline as you move forward. By integrating strategies such as routine building, delaying gratification, and practicing self-awareness, you can strengthen your discipline and set yourself up for continued success. Whether in your personal life, academic pursuits, or career, discipline is the key to unlocking your full potential and achieving lasting fulfillment.

Trust and Character Development: A Crucial Interrelationship

Understanding Trust in Interpersonal Relationships

As a therapist, I deal with deeply personal and often complex issues that clients bring into our sessions. One of the first things I do when beginning a relationship with a new client is to read a confidentiality statement. This assurance—that everything they share about their past or current experiences is kept strictly confidential—establishes a foundation of trust. The only exceptions to this confidentiality are when a client discloses intentions to harm themselves or reveals experiences of abuse, situations that I am legally obligated to report as a mandated reporter.

This seemingly simple statement of confidentiality is, in fact, a cornerstone of trust. It's remarkable how clients, after hearing this assurance, often feel more comfortable sharing profoundly personal experiences. The level of trust varies from client to client; some may withhold sensitive information for years, not because they fear I will share it, but because they are not yet ready to be vulnerable. Over time, as they engage in the therapeutic process and observe how I handle smaller disclosures, they gradually decide when it's the right time to share more. This journey illustrates that trust isn't solely built over years—it can develop rapidly or slowly, and just as it can be built, it can also be eroded, whether quickly or gradually.

Often, people hesitate to be vulnerable because they're

unsure how the other person will react or handle the information. They may fear that their disclosures are too burdensome, or they may have had past experiences where their trust was betrayed. This hesitation underscores the delicate nature of trust in relationships, whether therapeutic, personal, or professional.

Trust, as defined by the American Psychological Association (APA), is the reliance on or confidence in the dependability of someone or something. In interpersonal relationships, trust signifies the confidence that one person or group has in another's reliability—specifically, their predictability in doing what they say they will do. This predictability is often more crucial than the intrinsic honesty of the other party. Trust is foundational to mature relationships, encompassing intimate, social, and professional interactions.

Components of Trust: A Framework for Character Development

Trust is built on several key elements: benevolence, integrity, competence, and predictability. These components are essential in the development of one's character and the foundation of strong, enduring relationships:

Benevolence: The perception that the trustee has the trustor's best interests at heart.

Integrity: Adherence to a set of principles that the trustor finds acceptable.

Competence: The trustee's ability to perform the tasks they are entrusted with.

Predictability: The consistency of the trustee's behavior, reinforcing the trustor's confidence over time.

In my work as a therapist, these components are constantly at play. For example, benevolence is demonstrated through genuine care and concern for the well-being of my clients, while integrity is maintained by upholding confidentiality and ethical standards. Competence is shown through my professional expertise and the ability to guide clients effectively, and predictability is reinforced by consistently providing a safe and supportive environment.

The Role of Trust in Character Development

Character development is deeply intertwined with trust, as trust is both a reflection of one's character and a determinant of how one's character is perceived by others. Developing a trustworthy character involves cultivating these components of trust: demonstrating benevolence by showing genuine care for others, maintaining integrity by adhering to ethical principles, building competence through continuous self-improvement, and ensuring predictability by being consistent in actions and decisions.

In therapy, trust is not just a tool for effective treatment but a mirror of the therapist's character. The way I handle confidential information, respond to disclosures, and support clients through their vulnerabilities directly impacts how they perceive my character. Over time, this trust builds a strong therapeutic alliance, which is crucial for the effectiveness of therapy.

Trust and Leadership

Steve Jobs, a visionary leader known for his influence on technology and design, emphasized the importance of trust in effective leadership. According to Jobs, trust is a crucial element that enables leaders to empower their teams and foster a culture of excellence and innovation. He believed that when leaders trust their team members, they allow them the autonomy to excel and take ownership of their work, which in turn drives success.

Three Key Elements Essential to Building Trust and Influencing Others:

Character: Jobs believed that integrity and consistency in actions are foundational to gaining trust. Leaders who act with integrity and stay true to their values, even when faced with difficult decisions, earn the trust and respect of their teams. This aligns with biblical teachings, such as Proverbs 11:3, which states, "The integrity of the upright guides them, but the unfaithful are destroyed by their duplicity." Integrity is crucial for maintaining trust, as it ensures that a leader's actions are consistent with their values.

Influence: Trust is the cornerstone of influence. Jobs asserted that when people trust a leader, they are more likely to follow their guidance and support their decisions. Influence is strengthened when a leader's actions align with their words, and when they demonstrate reliability and honesty. Proverbs 3:5-6 reinforces this idea, urging believers to "Trust in the Lord with all your heart and lean not on your own understanding; in all your ways submit to him, and he will make your paths straight." Just as trust in God guides believers, trust in leadership guides teams.

Competence: Jobs also stressed that trust hinges on a leader's competence. A leader must demonstrate knowledge and expertise in their field to inspire confidence in their team. Competence, coupled with trust, drives results and fosters a high-performing team. This reflects the biblical principle found in Proverbs 16:3, "Commit to the Lord whatever you do, and he will establish your plans." Competence, rooted in trust, is essential for achieving success and fulfilling one's purpose.

Trust Judgments and First Impressions

Research shows that trust judgments are often made almost instantaneously—within just 100 milliseconds—based on facial appearance and other non-verbal cues. This rapid assessment underscores the importance of first impressions in trust development. Once established, trust becomes a crucial aspect of relationship building, but if broken, it is challenging to restore. This highlights the need for mindfulness in how one presents themselves and interacts with others, as these initial interactions can have long-lasting impacts on relationships and character.

Warmth vs. Competence in Trust Formation

When deciding whether to trust someone, people generally prioritize warmth over competence. Warmth encompasses qualities like kindness, empathy, and benevolence, which are essential for establishing trust. Competence, while important, is often secondary because trust is fundamentally an emotional judgment. This preference for warmth over competence suggests that in character development, fostering qualities that convey genuine care and empathy towards others is crucial for being perceived as trustworthy.

The Neuroscience of Trust

Neuroscientific research has shown that different brain networks are involved in conditional and unconditional trust. Conditional trust relies on continuous evaluation of the trustee's actions, while unconditional trust is more stable and less dependent on ongoing assessments. This distinction is important for understanding how trust operates on both cognitive and emotional levels. Trust involves complex brain processes that bind representations of the self, others, the situation, and emotions into a coherent pattern known as a semantic pointer. This integration allows for efficient and biologically feasible trust judgments.

Oxytocin, often referred to as the "love hormone," has been studied for its role in social bonding and trust. While its effects on trust are still debated, some research suggests that oxytocin may enhance feelings of trust and social bonding, contributing to the emotional dimension of trust. This connection between trust and neurochemistry highlights the biological underpinnings of trust and its role in shaping human relationships.

Trust in Character Development: Practical Applications

Building and Maintaining Trust:

Developing a trustworthy character involves consistently demonstrating the components of trust—benevolence, integrity, competence, and predictability. This requires conscious effort in all interactions, whether personal or professional, to ensure that others perceive you as reliable and trustworthy.

Self-Awareness and Trust:

Self-awareness is crucial in understanding how others perceive your actions and decisions. By being mindful of your behavior and the signals you send, you can better manage how you are perceived and ensure that you are building trust rather than eroding it.

The Importance of Warmth:

Since warmth is often prioritized over competence in trust judgments, developing a character that is perceived as warm and empathetic is vital. This can be achieved by cultivating qualities such as kindness, empathy, and a genuine interest in the well-being of others.

The Role of Integrity:

Integrity is foundational to trust. Adhering to ethical principles and being consistent in your actions fosters a perception of reliability. This consistency is crucial for maintaining long-term trust, especially in situations where others rely on you.

Trust in Professional Settings:

In professional environments, trust is often built through a combination of competence and warmth. While businesses tend to emphasize competence, it is essential not to overlook the importance of warmth, as it is crucial for building lasting trust with clients, colleagues, and stakeholders.

Trust as a Cornerstone of Character Development

Trust is a fundamental aspect of character development, influencing how individuals are perceived and how they interact with others. By understanding the components of trust and the factors that influence trust judgments, individuals can develop a trustworthy character that fosters strong, healthy relationships. Whether in personal life or professional settings, cultivating trust through benevolence, integrity, competence, and predictability is essential for long-term success and fulfillment.

Strategies to Build Trust

Building trust is a multifaceted process that requires intentional effort, consistency, and authenticity. Research and practical strategies suggest several ways to cultivate trust in both personal and professional relationships. Here are some evidence-based approaches:

1. Consistency and Reliability

According to research on trust, consistency in behavior is a key factor in building trust. When individuals consistently follow through on their commitments, they are perceived as more reliable and trustworthy.

- **Practical Application**: Be reliable by doing what you say you will do. Show up on time, meet deadlines, and maintain consistency in your actions and decisions. This builds a reputation of dependability, which is foundational to trust.

2. Open and Honest Communication

Studies in communication psychology emphasize that transparency and honesty are crucial for building trust. People are more likely to trust individuals who communicate openly, even when delivering bad news.

- **Practical Application**: Be transparent in your communication. Share relevant information openly and honestly, and admit when you don't have all the answers. Avoid hiding information or being overly secretive, as this can erode trust.

3. Active Listening

Active listening, which involves fully concentrating, understanding, responding, and then remembering what is being said, is shown to be effective in building trust. It shows that you value the other person's perspective.

- **Practical Application**: Practice active listening by giving your full attention during conversations, asking clarifying questions, and reflecting back what the other person has said. This demonstrates respect and builds trust by showing that you care about their thoughts and feelings.

4. Empathy and Emotional Intelligence

Emotional intelligence, particularly the ability to empathize with others, is strongly linked to trust-building. Empathy helps in understanding others' emotions and responding appropriately, which fosters trust.

- **Practical Application**: Cultivate empathy by trying to understand situations from others' perspectives and responding with compassion. Acknowledge and validate their feelings, which can build deeper connections and trust.

5. Demonstrating Competence

Trust in professional settings often hinges on perceived competence. When individuals demonstrate expertise and the ability to perform tasks effectively, they earn trust.

- **Practical Application**: Continuously develop your skills and knowledge in your field. Share your expertise when appropriate, and deliver high-quality work consistently. Competence, combined with other trust-building behaviors, solidifies trust in professional relationships.

6. Benevolence and Altruism

Benevolence, or the genuine concern for others' well-being, is a key component of trust. People are more likely to trust those who they believe have their best interests at heart.

- **Practical Application**: Show benevolence by offering help without expecting anything in return, being supportive during others' times of need, and showing kindness in your interactions. This can build trust by reinforcing the idea that you are looking out for others' best interests.

7. Admitting Mistakes

Admitting mistakes rather than covering them up can actually enhance trust. Research shows that people are more likely to trust those who are honest about their errors and take responsibility for their actions.

- **Practical Application**: When you make a mistake, admit it promptly and take corrective action. Apologize sincerely and outline the steps you will take to prevent similar issues in the future. This demonstrates integrity and fosters trust.

8. Building a Reputation for Fairness

Fairness and justice in interactions are crucial for trust. Studies suggest that people trust individuals and organizations more when they perceive them as fair and just.

- **Practical Application**: Treat everyone with respect and fairness, regardless of their status or role. Make decisions based on principles of equity and justice, and ensure that others see that you are fair in your dealings.

9. Setting Clear Expectations

Clear communication about expectations helps prevent misunderstandings and builds trust. When expectations are understood and met, it reinforces reliability.

- **Practical Application**: Clearly articulate your expectations in both personal and professional settings. Ensure that everyone involved understands their roles and responsibilities and follow up to ensure these expectations are met.

10. Creating Opportunities for Mutual Success

Collaboration and shared success are powerful trust-builders. Research shows that people are more likely to trust those with whom they have successfully collaborated on projects or goals.

- **Practical Application**: Foster opportunities for collaboration where both parties can achieve mutual benefits. Celebrate shared successes and acknowledge each person's contributions, which can strengthen the trust between collaborators.

11. Building Trust Through Small Wins

Trust is often built gradually through small, positive interactions. Research indicates that small, consistent behaviors that align with trustworthiness contribute significantly to long-term trust.

- **Practical Application**: Start by building trust through small, reliable actions. Whether it's delivering on a small task or consistently being supportive, these small wins accumulate over time, establishing a strong foundation of trust.

12. Cultural Sensitivity and Adaptability

Understanding and respecting cultural differences is essential in diverse environments. Trust is more likely to develop when individuals show cultural sensitivity and adaptability.

- **Practical Application**: Be aware of cultural differences in your interactions and be willing to adapt your behavior accordingly. Showing respect for others' cultural norms and practices can build trust in multicultural settings.

13. Managing Expectations in Conflict

How conflict is managed plays a crucial role in trust. Research suggests that handling conflict with honesty, respect, and a focus on resolution builds trust, even in challenging situations.

- **Practical Application**: Approach conflicts with a focus on resolution rather than winning. Be honest about the issues, listen to the other person's perspective, and work towards a solution that is fair and acceptable to all parties involved.

By implementing these strategies, you can effectively build and maintain trust in both personal and professional relationships, fostering environments where individuals feel valued, respected, and secure.

Celebrating Milestones: Acknowledging Your Achievements

Reaching milestones is a significant part of any journey, whether personal or professional. Celebrating these achievements is not merely about acknowledging success; it's about reinforcing the behaviors and decisions that led to these successes. Each milestone is a testament to your hard work, perseverance, and the effectiveness of the strategies you've employed.

The Importance of Acknowledging Achievements

- **Boosts Motivation:** Celebrating successes, no matter how small, provides motivation to keep going.
- **Builds Confidence:** Acknowledging accomplishments helps build self-confidence and a sense of competence.
- **Reinforces Positive Behavior:** Recognition reinforces the behaviors and actions that led to success.
- **Provides a Sense of Progress:** Celebrating milestones gives a tangible sense of progress, making long-term goals feel more achievable.
- **Encourages Persistence:** Recognizing achievements helps maintain persistence in the face of challenges and setbacks.

Strategies for Acknowledging Achievements

- **Set Clear Milestones:** Break down your larger goals into smaller, achievable milestones. This makes it easier to track progress and celebrate successes.

- **Create a Reward System:** Develop a reward system for achieving milestones. Rewards can be small, such as taking a break, or larger, such as treating yourself to something special.

- **Reflect on Progress:** Regularly reflect on your progress and accomplishments. Journaling can be a useful tool for this.

- **Share Your Successes:** Share your achievements with friends, family, or colleagues. Celebrating together can enhance the sense of accomplishment.

- **Celebrate in a Meaningful Way:** Choose celebrations that are meaningful to you. This could be a quiet moment of reflection, a celebratory meal, or an activity you enjoy.

- **Visualize Your Success:** Create a visual representation of your achievements, such as a progress chart or vision board. This serves as a constant reminder of your progress.

- **Express Gratitude:** Practice gratitude by acknowledging the support and contributions of others in your successes.

Celebrating and Sustaining Progress

As you celebrate your milestones, remember that your gifts, passions, and talents will open doors for you, but it is your character that will sustain you and ensure long-term success. The character traits you've cultivated are the keys to not only achieving but sustaining success. You've recognized your extraordinary potential; now, with the solid foundation of character you've built, go forth and achieve the impossible.

Tools and Techniques for Acknowledging Achievements

- **Journaling:** Keep a journal to document your progress, achievements, and reflections.
- Progress Charts: Use charts or graphs to track your milestones and progress visually.
- **Vision Boards:** Create a vision board with images and words representing your goals and achievements.
- **Gratitude Lists:** Regularly write down things you are grateful for, including your achievements and progress.
- **Celebration Rituals:** Develop personal rituals for celebrating milestones, such as a favorite meal or a particular activity.

Sustaining Progress: Maintaining Momentum Over Time

J ust as a car or house needs regular maintenance, your personal and professional skills require continuous development to sustain the progress you've made. Engaging with environments that stimulate growth—such as reading, networking, and participating in meaningful social engagements —is necessary to maintain your achievements. Any progress that is not maintained is bound to diminish over time.

Giving back through teaching or serving your community is one of the most profound ways to sustain progress. For me, working in the mental and behavioral health field as a counselor and therapist, and volunteering in my local church, have been instrumental in sustaining my progress. Serving others, especially young people, has kept me focused and grounded in my purpose.

The Importance of Sustaining Momentum

- **Maintains Progress:** Sustaining momentum helps maintain the progress you've made towards your goals.
- **Builds Consistency:** Developing habits and routines fosters consistency, which is key to achieving long-term success.
- **Encourages Continuous Improvement:** Regularly evaluating and adjusting your approach promotes continuous improvement.

- **Enhances Resilience:** Sustaining momentum builds resilience, enabling you to navigate challenges and setbacks more effectively.
- **Fosters Adaptability:** Adapting to changes and new information ensures that you stay on track towards your goals.

Strategies for Sustaining Momentum

- **Develop Effective Habits:** Identify and cultivate habits that support your goals. Focus on one habit at a time until it becomes automatic.
- **Create Routines:** Establish daily, weekly, and monthly routines that incorporate activities aligned with your goals.
- **Set Regular Check-Ins:** Schedule regular check-ins to assess your progress, adjust your approach, and set new targets.
- **Stay Focused on Your Why:** Keep your ultimate goals and reasons for pursuing them at the forefront of your mind. This helps maintain motivation and direction.
- **Embrace Flexibility:** Be willing to adjust your plans and strategies as needed. Flexibility allows you to adapt to new challenges and opportunities.
- **Seek Support:** Surround yourself with supportive people who encourage and motivate you. This can include mentors, peers, and accountability partners.

- **Celebrate Small Wins:** Regularly celebrate small achievements to maintain a sense of progress and motivation.

Tools and Techniques for Sustaining Momentum

- **Habit Trackers:** Use habit-tracking tools to monitor and reinforce your habits.
- **Calendars and Planners:** Schedule your routines and check-ins using calendars and planners.
- **Accountability Partners:** Partner with someone who can hold you accountable and provide support.
- **Mindfulness Practices:** Incorporate mindfulness practices such as meditation or journaling to stay focused and reflective.
- **Continuous Learning:** Engage in continuous learning to stay motivated and adaptable.

Giving Back: The Role of Service in Personal Growth

Giving back involves sharing your knowledge, experiences, and resources with others. It is about using your God-given talents and abilities to make a difference in the world. God has blessed each of us with unique gifts and talents (1 Corinthians 12:4-7), and when we use these gifts for His glory, we not only fulfill our purpose but also build our self-confidence and self-esteem. This fosters a culture of growth and inspiration within your community, contributing to your personal fulfillment and the development of others.

The Importance of Giving Back

- **Creates a Positive Impact:** Giving back positively impacts others and your community.
- **Fosters Personal Growth:** Sharing your knowledge and experiences helps you grow personally and professionally.
- **Builds a Supportive Network:** Giving back strengthens your connections and builds a supportive network.
- **Enhances Fulfillment:** Contributing to others' growth and success brings a sense of fulfillment and purpose.
- **Encourages a Culture of Growth:** By giving back, you promote a culture of continuous learning and development within your community.

Strategies for Giving Back

- **Mentorship:** Offer mentorship to those who can benefit from your experience and knowledge.
- **Volunteering:** Volunteer your time and skills to organizations and causes you care about.
- **Sharing Knowledge:** Share your knowledge through writing, speaking, or teaching.
- **Supporting Others:** Provide support and encouragement to others pursuing their goals.
- **Creating Opportunities:** Create opportunities for others by offering internships, workshops, or collaborative projects.

- **Promoting Inclusivity:** Advocate for inclusivity and diversity within your community and networks.
- **Leading by Example:** Lead by example through your actions and commitment to personal and community growth.

Tools and Techniques for Giving Back

- **Mentorship Programs:** Participate in or establish mentorship programs within your community or organization.
- **Volunteer Platforms:** Use volunteer platforms to find opportunities to contribute your skills and time.
- **Workshops and Seminars:** Organize or participate in workshops and seminars to share your knowledge.
- **Networking Events:** Attend networking events to connect with and support others.
- **Online Communities:** Engage in online communities and forums to share insights and offer support.

Avoiding Negative Outlets and Embracing Continuous Growth

Purposefully avoiding negative outlets and influences is crucial in sustaining progress. When I became aware of my true calling and set clear goals, I made the necessary changes to stay on track. Connecting with my local church through volunteering helped me avoid negative influences and maintain focus on my goals. While many of my peers sought short-term gratification, I remained committed to my purpose, understanding the long-term consequences of my choices. This practice of self-discipline allowed me to stay on track, pursue my long-term goals, and avoid distractions that could derail my progress.

Sustaining progress also involves continuous learning and personal growth. By engaging in ongoing professional development, reading, and serving others, you ensure that your progress is maintained and enhanced over time. This commitment to growth helps you stay ahead, adapt to new challenges, and continue moving forward with purpose and intention.

Call to Action

As you stand at the threshold of sustained success, take a moment to reflect on the milestones you've achieved and the growth you've experienced throughout this journey. Now, consider how you can extend this success beyond yourself. Use the resilience, adaptability, humility, integrity, perseverance, self-discipline, and trust you've developed to make a meaningful difference in the lives of others. Whether through mentorship, volunteering, or simply sharing your story, your journey continues as you help others to navigate their paths. Remember, true success is not just about what you accomplish—it's about how you use your achievements to uplift those around you.

Conclusion of Step 7: Embrace Growth and Pay It Forward

D eveloping character, celebrating milestones, maintaining momentum, and giving back are essential components of achieving and sustaining extraordinary success. The character traits you've cultivated—resilience, adaptability, humility, integrity, perseverance, self-discipline, and trust—serve as the foundation upon which your lasting success is built. By acknowledging and celebrating your achievements, you reinforce the positive behaviors that have guided you, fueling your continued progress.

Maintaining momentum requires a commitment to ongoing growth and adaptability, ensuring that your journey doesn't end with reaching a goal but continues as you evolve and set new aspirations. Most importantly, giving back by sharing your knowledge, experiences, and strengths with others not only solidifies your success but also creates a ripple effect of empowerment and inspiration. Through these practices, you truly recognize and harness your extraordinary potential, leaving a lasting impact on the world around you and helping others achieve their impossible dreams.

Remember, you can bake the finest cake in the world, but if it isn't properly cooked, your guests won't enjoy it, leaving your time and energy wasted. Just as with baking, it's the thoroughness of your character development that ensures your success is truly fulfilling and appreciated by others.

Activity 1: Achievement Reflection Journal

Purpose: Regularly reflecting on and celebrating accomplishments to maintain motivation and confidence

Instructions:

Daily Reflection: At the end of each day, write down three things you accomplished. These can be big or small achievements.

Weekly Summary: At the end of each week, review your daily reflections and summarize your significant achievements for the week.

Monthly Reflection: At the end of each month, review your weekly summaries and reflect on your progress towards your long-term goals.

Milestone Celebration: Identify significant milestones you have achieved and plan a celebration to acknowledge your hard work.

Solution:

Daily Reflection Example:

"Completed a challenging project at work."

"Helped a colleague with their task."

"Maintained a positive attitude throughout the day."

Weekly Summary Example:

"This week, I finished the project, assisted my team, and kept a positive outlook despite stress."

Monthly Reflection Example:

"Over the past month, I completed multiple projects, received positive feedback from my supervisor, and managed my stress effectively."

Milestone Celebration Example:

"Reached a major project milestone. I will celebrate by taking a day off to relax and enjoy a favorite activity."

Activity 2: Habit and Routine Development Plan

Purpose: Develop habits and routines that support ongoing progress and continuous improvement.

Instructions:

Identify Key Areas: List the key areas in your life where you want to sustain momentum (e.g., health, career, personal development).

Set Specific Habits: For each key area, identify specific habits that will help you make progress. Ensure these habits are actionable and measurable.

Create a Routine: Develop a daily or weekly routine that incorporates these habits.

Track Progress: Use a habit tracker to monitor your adherence to these routines and reflect on your progress regularly.

Solution:

Key Areas Example:

Health: Exercise, nutrition, sleep.

Career: Skill development, networking, productivity.

Personal Development: Reading, meditation, journaling.

Specific Habits Example:

Health: Exercise for 30 minutes daily, eat three balanced meals, and sleep 7-8 hours nightly.

Career: Spend 1 hour daily on skill development, attend one networking event weekly, and use a planner to organize tasks.

Personal Development: Read for 20 minutes daily, meditate for 10 minutes daily, journal every evening.

Routine Example:

Morning: Exercise, meditate, and plan the day.
Afternoon: Work on skill development and complete work tasks.
Evening: Reflect on the day, read, journal.

Progress Tracking Example:

Use a habit tracker app or a bullet journal to check off completed habits each day.

Review the tracker at the end of each week to assess consistency and make adjustments as needed.

Activity 3: Community Contribution Plan

Purpose: Sharing knowledge and experiences with others to foster a culture of growth and inspiration.

Instructions:

Identify Your Strengths: Reflect on your areas of expertise and experiences that could benefit others.

Choose Contribution Methods:

Decide how you want to share your knowledge (e.g., mentoring, writing articles, giving talks).

Set Contribution Goals:

Establish specific goals for contributing to your community (e.g., mentor one person per month, write one article per week).

Track Impact: Keep a record of your contributions and reflect on the impact they have on others.

Solution:

Identify Your Strengths Example:

"I have strong skills in project management and public speaking."

Contribution Methods Example:

"I will mentor junior colleagues, write blog posts on project management, and give talks at local community centers."

Contribution Goals Example:

"Mentor one junior colleague per month, write one blog post per week, and give one talk per quarter."

Track Impact Example:

"Keep a journal of mentoring sessions, collect feedback from blog readers, and record audience responses from talks."

Assessment and Reflection

Purpose: Assess the effectiveness of your efforts and reflect on your growth.

Instructions:

Quarterly Review: Conduct a quarterly review of your achievement reflections, habit tracker, and community contributions.

Self-Assessment: Assess your progress in each key area and identify what worked well and what needs improvement.

Adjust Goals: Adjust your goals and routines based on your self-assessment to ensure continuous improvement.
Solution:

Quarterly Review Example:

"Review journal entries, habit tracker, and contribution records from the past three months."

Self-Assessment Example:

"In the health area, I consistently exercised and slept well but need to improve nutrition."
"In my career, I made significant progress in skill development but need to network more."
"In personal development, I maintained my reading habit but need to be more consistent with meditation."

Adjust Goals Example:

"For health, plan and prepare balanced meals weekly."
"For career, attend two networking events per month."
"For personal development, set a specific time for daily meditation."

Conclusion: Unleashing Your Extraordinary Future

C ongratulations on completing *The Extraordinary Within: A 7-Step Guide to Recognizing Your Potential and Achieving the Impossible*. This journey has been about more than just reading a book—it's about transforming your life by embracing the extraordinary potential within you. Each step in this guide has been designed to build upon the last, equipping you with the tools, mindset, and strategies necessary to achieve the impossible. As you move forward, remember that this journey is ongoing, and your potential is limitless.

Recap of Key Strategies

Step 1: Discovering Your Hidden Potential

Recap: Discovering your hidden potential is the cornerstone of your journey. By identifying your strengths and embracing a growth mindset, you set the foundation for unlocking the extraordinary within you. This step is about realizing that your abilities can be developed through perseverance and learning, allowing you to embark on a path toward remarkable achievements.

Key Takeaway: Recognize that your potential is not

fixed but can be expanded through continuous growth and self-discovery.

Step 2: Overcoming Limiting Beliefs, Thoughts, and Building Confidence

Recap: Overcoming limiting beliefs and negative thoughts is crucial for unlocking your full potential. This step emphasizes the importance of recognizing and transforming the self-imposed barriers that hold you back. By building self-confidence and reframing your mindset, you empower yourself to pursue your goals with resilience and determination.

Key Takeaway: Challenge the beliefs that limit you and replace them with empowering thoughts that propel you toward success.

Step 3: Identifying Purpose, Goal Setting, and Vision Crafting

Recap: Identifying your purpose, setting SMART goals, and crafting a clear vision are essential for directing your efforts and sustaining motivation. This step helps you align your actions with your deeper purpose, ensuring that every goal you set brings you closer to achieving your extraordinary potential.

Key Takeaway: A well-defined purpose and clear goals provide the roadmap for your journey toward success.

Step 4: Time Management, Prioritization, and Continuous Learning

Recap: Effective time management, prioritization, and continuous learning are critical for maintaining momentum on your journey. This step teaches you how to allocate your time wisely, focus on what truly matters, and remain adaptable in an ever-changing world. By mastering these skills, you create a sustainable framework for ongoing personal and professional growth.

Key Takeaway: Manage your time and priorities effectively while committing to lifelong learning to stay ahead and achieve the extraordinary.

Step 5: Networking, Mentorship, and Support Systems

Recap: Building strong networks, finding mentors, and creating support systems are vital for achieving lasting success. This step highlights the importance of surrounding yourself with positive influences and nurturing relationships that provide guidance, opportunities, and encouragement.

Key Takeaway: Engage with mentors and a supportive network to navigate challenges and leverage growth opportunities.

Step 6: Resilience, Learning from Failure, and Embracing Risk

Recap: Resilience, learning from failure, and embracing

risk are fundamental to overcoming obstacles and achieving your goals. This step encourages you to view failures as learning opportunities and to take calculated risks that push you beyond your comfort zone, fostering growth and innovation.

Key Takeaway: Embrace resilience and a willingness to take risks as you navigate your path toward success.

Step 7: Developing Character, Celebrating Milestones, and Sustaining Progress

Recap: Developing character, celebrating milestones, and sustaining progress are crucial for maintaining momentum and achieving lasting success. This final step emphasizes the importance of recognizing your achievements, cultivating habits that foster continuous growth, and contributing to the development of others.

Key Takeaway: Regularly celebrate your progress, sustain your momentum, and focus on continuous character development while giving back to others. This creates a cycle of growth and fulfillment that strengthens your journey and positively impacts those around you.

Achieving the Impossible: Embrace Your Unique Journey

As you continue on your journey, remember that achieving the impossible requires embracing your unique path. Each step you take, each challenge you overcome, and each success you celebrate contributes to your extraordinary future. Here are key principles to keep in mind as you move forward:

- **Embrace Your Uniqueness:** Recognize your strengths, value your experiences, and trust your instincts. These are valuable guides on your journey.
- **Defy the Status Quo:** Challenge conventional thinking, take calculated risks, and stay true to your vision, even in the face of doubt.
- **Continue Learning and Growing:** Commit to lifelong learning, adapt and evolve, and seek feedback to improve and stay on track.
- **Foster a Growth-Oriented Community:** Share your knowledge, support others, and celebrate collective success to create a thriving environment for everyone.

ACKNOWLEDGEMENTS

To my beloved wife, Pheona—your unwavering support and countless conversations have been the wellspring of inspiration for this book. Your insights, ideas, and living example have deeply influenced the discussions and reflections shared here. Thank you for standing by me, encouraging me, and believing in this journey with me.

To my family, especially my mother, Doris Ayeni, and my father, McDonald Ayeni—your encouragement and continued support have been my motivation to keep writing. Your love and belief in me have been a constant source of strength. To my in-laws, especially my mother-in-law, Carmen Thompson—thank you for your support and for being an extended family that nurtures and uplifts me.

To my spiritual father and mentor, Rev. Dr. Wisdom Okotie—your guidance, prayers, and spiritual wisdom sustain me daily. I am deeply grateful for your mentorship, which has been pivotal in my personal and professional growth.

To my friend Patrick Jones, my "gentle scholar"—from the start of graduate school to our ongoing professional journey, your companionship and intellectual exchanges have been invaluable. We have empowered each other through shared ideas and mutual support, and I am thankful for your presence in my life.

To my daughter, Naomi—your story of grit, determination, and resilience inspired me profoundly. It served as a teaching point in this book and is a testament to the power of perseverance.

To Lara and the dedicated team of experts, professional editors, and marketers at Legacy Lantern Publishing House—this book would not have come to life without your tireless efforts. Your expertise and commitment have been instrumental in bringing this project to fruition.

Finally, to all those who continue to encourage and cheer me on—whether we've met or are yet to meet, your kind words and support mean more than you know. Thank you for being a part of this journey.

BIBLIOGRAPHY

Bandura, A. (1986). Social Foundations of Thought and Action: A Social Cognitive Theory. Prentice-Hall.

Bandura, A. (1997). Self-Efficacy: The Exercise of Control. W.H. Freeman.

Brehm, J. W. (1966). A Theory of Psychological Reactance. Academic Press.

Brown, B. (2012). Daring Greatly: How the Courage to Be Vulnerable Transforms the Way We Live, Love, Parent, and Lead. Avery.

Burns, D. D. (1999). Feeling Good: The New Mood Therapy. Harper.

Clear, J. (2018). Atomic Habits: An Easy & Proven Way to Build Good Habits & Break Bad Ones. Avery.

Covey, S. R. (1989). The 7 Habits of Highly Effective People: Powerful Lessons in Personal Change. Free Press.

Csikszentmihalyi, M. (1990). Flow: The Psychology of Optimal Experience. Harper & Row.

Diener, E., Lucas, R. E., & Scollon, C. N. (2006). Beyond the hedonic treadmill: Revising the adaptation theory of well-being. American Psychologist, 61(4), 305-314.

Duckworth, A. L. (2016). Grit: The Power of Passion and Perseverance. Scribner.

Duckworth, A. L., & Quinn, P. D. (2009). Development

and validation of the Short Grit Scale (GRIT–S). Journal of Personality Assessment, 91(2), 166-174.

Duckworth, A. L., Peterson, C., Matthews, M. D., & Kelly, D. R. (2007). Grit: Perseverance and passion for long-term goals. Journal of Personality and Social Psychology, 92(6), 1087-1101.

Dweck, C. S. (2006). Mindset: The New Psychology of Success. Random House.

Ellis, A. (1994). Reason and Emotion in Psychotherapy. Citadel Press.

Fredrickson, B. L. (2009). Positivity: Top-Notch Research Reveals the Upward Spiral That Will Change Your Life. Crown.

Future proof: Solving the adaptability paradox for the long-term. (n.d.). McKinsey & Company.

Gladwell, M. (2000). The Tipping Point: How Little Things Can Make a Big Difference. Little, Brown.

Goleman, D. (1995). Emotional Intelligence: Why It Can Matter More Than IQ. Bantam Books.

Goodwin, D. K. (2005). Team of Rivals: The Political Genius of Abraham Lincoln. Simon & Schuster.

Grant, A. M. (2013). Give and Take: A Revolutionary Approach to Success. Viking.

How to persevere. (n.d.). University of Washington.

Integrity in the workplace. (n.d.). PositivePsychology.com.

Isaacson, W. (2011). Steve Jobs. Simon & Schuster.

Janis, I. L. (1972). Victims of Groupthink: A Psychological

Study of Foreign-Policy Decisions and Fiascoes. Houghton Mifflin.

Kaufman, S. B. (2013). Ungifted: Intelligence Redefined. Basic Books.

Langer, E. J. (2014). Mindfulness. Da Capo Lifelong Books.

Latham, G. P., & Locke, E. A. (2007). New developments and directions for goal-setting research are needed. European Psychologist, 12(4), 290-300.

Locke, E. A., & Latham, G. P. (2002). Building a practically sound theory of goal setting and task motivation: A 35-year odyssey. American Psychologist, 57(9), 705-717.

Martin, A. J., & Marsh, H. W. (2007). Academic buoyancy: Towards an understanding of students' everyday academic resilience. Journal of School Psychology, 45(3), 269-282.

Merrill, D., & Merrill, R. (2003). First Things First: To Live, to Love, to Learn, to Leave a Legacy. Simon & Schuster.

Moffitt, T. E., Arseneault, L., Belsky, D., Dickson, N., Hancox, R. J., Harrington, H., ... & Caspi, A. (2011). A gradient of childhood self-control predicts health, wealth, and public safety. Proceedings of the National Academy of Sciences, 108(7), 2693-2698.

Neff, K. D. (2011). Self-Compassion: Stop Beating Yourself Up and Leave Insecurity Behind. HarperCollins.

Newport, C. (2016). Deep Work: Rules for Focused Success in a Distracted World. Grand Central Publishing.

Peterson, C., & Seligman, M. E. P. (2004). Character

strengths and virtues: A handbook and classification. Oxford University Press.

Pink, D. H. (2009). Drive: The Surprising Truth About What Motivates Us. Riverhead Books.

Promoting perseverance. (2024). Psychology Today.

Rath, T. (2007). StrengthsFinder 2.0. Gallup Press.

Robinson, K., & Aronica, L. (2009). The Element: How Finding Your Passion Changes Everything. Penguin Books.

Ryan, R. M., & Deci, E. L. (2000). Self-determination theory and the facilitation of intrinsic motivation, social development, and well-being. American Psychologist, 55(1), 68-78.

Schwantes, M. (2024). *Steve Jobs Pointed Out 1 Clear Sign to Spot Someone With Good Leadership Skills.* Inc.

Seligman, M. E. P. (1975). Helplessness: On Depression, Development, and Death. W.H. Freeman.

Seligman, M. E. P. (2011). Flourish: A Visionary New Understanding of Happiness and Well-being. Atria Books.

Sinek, S. (2009). Start with Why: How Great Leaders Inspire Everyone to Take Action. Portfolio.

Snyder, C. R. (2000). Handbook of Hope: Theory, Measures, and Applications. Academic Press.

Southwick, S. M., & Charney, D. S. (2012). The science of resilience: Implications for the prevention and treatment of depression. Science, 338(6103), 79-82.

Stajkovic, A. D., & Luthans, F. (1998). Self-efficacy and work-related performance: A meta-analysis. Psychological Bulletin, 124(2), 240-261.

Tangney, J. P. (2000). Humility: Theoretical perspectives, empirical findings, and directions for future research. Journal of Social and Clinical Psychology, 19(1), 70-82.

Thagard, P. (2018). *What Is Trust?* Psychology Today. Retrieved from https://www.psychologytoday.com/us/blog/hot-thought/201810/what-is-trust

Tharp, T., & Reiter, M. (2003). The Creative Habit: Learn It and Use It for Life. Simon & Schuster.

Travers, M. (2024). *A Psychologist Explains Where Our Trust Issues Really Come From.* Forbes.

Van Dierendonck, D. (2011). Servant leadership: A review and synthesis. Journal of Management, 37(4), 1228-1261.

Van Lange, P. A. M., & Balliet, D. (2015). *How and why humans trust: A meta-analysis and elaborated model. Behavioral and Brain Sciences,* 39, e15.

Vanderkam, L. (2010). 168 Hours: You Have More Time Than You Think. Portfolio.

Waytz, A. (2024). *Friend or Foe? A Psychological Perspective on Trust.* Kellogg School of Management.

Waytz, A. (2024). *Measuring Trust: Through Competence or Warmth?* Kellogg School of Management.

Waytz, A. (2024). *The Importance of First Impressions and Trust: Key Findings.* Kellogg School of Management.

Wertz, J. (2024, June 26). How to foster integrity as a core value in your leadership style. Forbes.

Zenger, J. H., & Folkman, J. (2009). The Extraordinary Leader: Turning Good Managers into Great Leaders. McGraw-Hill Education.

19 effective strategies for building a culture of adapt-ability. (2023). Forbes.

9 tips to help you strengthen your integrity. (n.d.). Success.

Scriptures

RESOURCES AND FURTHER READING

Books and Articles

Bernhard, T. (2020). *How Distorted Thinking Increases Stress and Anxiety.* Psychology Today.
Explains the role of cognitive distortions in contributing to mental health issues like anxiety and depression.

Brown, B. (2012). *Daring Greatly: How the Courage to Be Vulnerable Transforms the Way We Live, Love, Parent, and Lead.* Penguin.
Brown explores the concept of vulnerability and how embracing it can lead to greater courage and a more fulfilling life.

Brown, B. (2013). *The Power of Vulnerability.* Sounds True.
Discusses the importance of embracing vulnerability as a source of strength and courage.

Clear, J. (2018). *Atomic Habits: An Easy & Proven Way to Build Good Habits & Break Bad Ones.* Avery.
A practical guide that delves into the power of small, consistent actions that can lead to significant changes over time.

Covey, S. R. (1989). *The 7 Habits of Highly Effective People: Powerful Lessons in Personal Change.* Free Press.
Covey's classic work on personal effectiveness offers timeless principles for personal and professional success.

Duhigg, C. (2012). *The Power of Habit: Why We Do What*

We Do in Life and Business. Random House.

Examines the science behind why habits exist and how they can be changed, offering practical strategies for transforming habits and achieving goals.

Duckworth, A. L. (2016). *Grit: The Power of Passion and Perseverance.* Scribner.

Explores the role of grit—passion and perseverance—in achieving long-term success.

Frankl, V. E. (1946). *Man's Search for Meaning.* Beacon Press.

A powerful memoir and psychological exploration of finding purpose even in the direst circumstances. Frankl's experiences as a Holocaust survivor emphasize the importance of purpose and meaning in life.

Gladwell, M. (2000). *The Tipping Point: How Little Things Can Make a Big Difference.* Little, Brown.

In this book, Gladwell indirectly touches upon forward-thinking strategies by showing how trends and innovations take root and how being ahead of the curve can lead to transformative change.

Goleman, D. (1995). *Emotional Intelligence: Why It Can Matter More Than IQ.* Bantam Books.

Examines the role of emotional intelligence in personal and professional success, with a focus on self-awareness, self-regulation, motivation, empathy, and social skills.

Heath, C., & Heath, D. (2010). *Switch: How to Change Things When Change Is Hard.* Broadway Books.

This book provides strategies for making lasting changes,

which is especially relevant to sustaining progress and adaptability in personal and organizational settings.

Locke, E. A., & Latham, G. P. (1990). *Goal Setting: A Motivational Technique that Works.* Prentice-Hall.

Introduces the goal-setting theory and its impact on motivation and performance.

Shenk, J. W. (2005). *Lincoln's Melancholy: How Depression Challenged a President and Fueled His Greatness.* Houghton Mifflin.

Provides insight into how Abraham Lincoln's struggles with depression contributed to his resilience and leadership.

Sinek, S. (2009). *Start With Why: How Great Leaders Inspire Everyone to Take Action.* Portfolio.

Sinek's groundbreaking book emphasizes the importance of understanding your "why"—your purpose—as the foundation for success and leadership.

Biblical Insights

Matthew 6:33 (pg. 30)

Emphasizes the importance of prioritizing spiritual growth and God's righteousness.

Acts 20:35 (pg. 30)

Highlights the joy and fulfillment found in serving others.

James 4:10 (pg. 30)

Teaches the value of humility and the promise that God will lift up those who humble themselves.

Matthew 6:19-20 (pg. 30)

Encourages the focus on storing treasures in heaven

rather than earthly possessions, emphasizing simplicity and eternal values.

Philippians 4:11 (pg. 30)

Illustrates the practice of contentment in any circumstance.

Jeremiah 29:11 (pg. 30, 70)

Reassures that God has a plan for our lives, filled with hope and a future.

Romans 5:3-5 (pg. 162)

Encourages a resilient mindset by explaining how suffering produces perseverance, character, and hope.

Hebrews 10:24-25 (pg. 138)

Stresses the importance of community and mutual encouragement in faith.

Proverbs 15:18 (pg. 75, 76)

Emphasizes the importance of patience and self-regulation in avoiding conflict.

John 1:12 (pg. 58)

Highlights the significance of understanding our identity as children of God, which is foundational to building self-confidence.

Romans 8:15-17 (pg. 58)

Reminds us of our identity as heirs with Christ, providing a deep sense of purpose and belonging.

Romans 8:38-39 (pg. 58)

Reassures us of God's unwavering love, which is the foundation of our self-worth and confidence.

Romans 12:2 (pg. 75, 76)

Encourages the renewal of the mind to align with God's will and purpose.

Matthew 18:4 (pg. 118, 119)

Illustrates the importance of humility in achieving greatness and fulfilling your purpose.

Proverbs 1:5 - (pg. 173)

Encourages the wise to listen and increase their learning, and the understanding to gain guidance, highlighting the importance of continuous learning and growth in character development.

James 1:2-4 - (pg. 175)

Urges believers to consider trials as opportunities for joy, knowing that the testing of their faith produces perseverance, which is essential for personal and spiritual growth.

Proverbs 20:25 - (pg. 187)

Warns against making rash decisions and emphasizes the importance of thoughtful consideration and discipline in achieving long-term success.

Colossians 3:23-24 - (pg. 189)

Encourages doing all work with sincerity and dedication as though working for the Lord, reinforcing the concept of integrity and self-discipline in daily life.

Proverbs 19:20 - (pg. 177)

Highlights the value of accepting advice and discipline, underscoring the role of humility and adaptability in achieving wisdom and success.

James 1:12 - (pg. 195)

Promises the crown of life to those who persevere under

trial, reinforcing the spiritual rewards of endurance and faithfulness.

Philippians 4:13 - (pg. 201)

Affirms that believers can do all things through Christ who strengthens them, offering encouragement and motivation to maintain self-discipline and perseverance.

Matthew 18:4 - (pg. 181)

Teaches that those who humble themselves like a child are the greatest in the kingdom of heaven, emphasizing the importance of humility in personal growth.

James 4:17 - (pg. 187)

Reminds us that knowing the right thing to do and failing to do it is sin, highlighting the significance of integrity and responsibility.

Proverbs 16:3 - (pg. 200)

Advises committing your work to the Lord, and your plans will be established, encouraging trust and perseverance in pursuing goals.

Galatians 6:9 - (pg. 195)

Encourages not to grow weary in doing good, for at the proper time we will reap a harvest if we do not give up, reinforcing the value of perseverance.

Proverbs 11:3 (pg. 207)

Affirms that integrity guides the upright, highlighting the importance of consistent ethical behavior in maintaining trust.

Proverbs 3:5-6 (pg. 207)

Encourages trust in the Lord as a guide for decision-making, illustrating the foundational role of trust in leading a righteous life.

Proverbs 16:3 (pg. 208)

Emphasizes committing one's work to the Lord and the establishment of plans, linking trust in divine guidance to personal and professional success.

Research and Reports

American Psychological Association (APA) on Resilience

Provides insights into the psychological concept of resilience and its role in adapting to adversity.

World Economic Forum: Future of Jobs Report

Highlights the importance of Emotional Intelligence and other key skills for the future workforce.

Websites and Online Courses

Coursera: Offers a wide range of online courses in personal development, psychology, leadership, and more. Perfect for those looking to engage in continuous learning.

MindsetWorks: A resource focused on cultivating a growth mindset, with tools and programs developed by Dr. Carol Dweck.

Udemy: Another platform offering diverse courses on various topics, from personal development to professional skills.

Gallup StrengthsFinder.

An online assessment tool that helps individuals identify their top strengths.

Inspirational Speeches

"I Have a Dream" by Dr. Martin Luther King Jr.

Dr. King's iconic speech, which remains a powerful example of purpose and vision in action.

Theodore Roosevelt's "Man in the Arena" Speech

A powerful excerpt from Roosevelt's speech, emphasizing the value of striving valiantly despite challenges.

NOTES

Step 1: Discovering Your Hidden Potential

Understanding Your Strengths:

Description: This section focuses on the importance of recognizing and acknowledging your unique strengths and talents. It covers techniques such as self-assessments, feedback from others, and reflecting on past successes to identify areas where you naturally excel.

Objective: To help readers gain a clear understanding of their innate abilities and how to leverage them for personal and professional growth.

Embracing a Growth Mindset:

Description: Here, readers are introduced to the concept of a growth mindset, as opposed to a fixed mindset. The section explains how a growth mindset fosters a love for learning, resilience in the face of challenges, and the belief that abilities can be developed over time.

Objective: To encourage readers to adopt a growth mindset, enabling them to view challenges as opportunities for growth rather than obstacles.

Setting Realistic Goals:

Description: This part of the chapter emphasizes the importance of setting specific, challenging, and attainable goals. It covers how realistic goals can provide direction, motivation, and a sense of accomplishment.

Objective: To equip readers with the tools to set effective goals that push them to grow without becoming overwhelmed.

Conclusion of Step 1:

Description: Summarizes the key points of discovering hidden potential and reinforces the idea that this discovery is just the beginning of a transformative journey.

Objective: To motivate readers to apply these insights and prepare for the next steps in their personal development.

Next Step Reference:

Description: Introduces the next step, which will focus on overcoming limiting beliefs, transforming negative thoughts, and building confidence.

Objective: To provide a smooth transition to the next chapter and highlight the importance of addressing internal barriers.

Step 2: Overcoming Limiting Beliefs, Thoughts, and Building Confidence

Understanding Beliefs and Their Impact on Individuals:

Description: This section delves into the nature of beliefs, how they are formed, and their profound influence on behavior, emotions, and decision-making. It discusses both empowering and limiting beliefs and how they shape one's self-perception and interactions with the world.

Objective: To help readers understand the deep-rooted nature of beliefs and the need to challenge those that are limiting.

Definition of Thoughts:

Description: Readers are introduced to the concept of thoughts as cognitive processes that interpret experiences and influence emotions and actions. The section differentiates between positive and negative thoughts, emphasizing the impact each has on well-being and behavior.

Objective: To make readers aware of the power of their thoughts and how they can consciously shape them to be more positive and constructive.

Positive vs. Negative Thoughts:

Description: This part compares and contrasts positive and negative thoughts, explaining how each type affects mental health, motivation, and overall outlook. It also introduces the idea of positive realistic thoughts, which balance optimism with practicality.

Objective: To encourage readers to shift from negative to positive realistic thoughts as a way to improve their mental and emotional resilience.

Relationship Between Thoughts and Beliefs:

Description: Explains the cyclical relationship between thoughts and beliefs, showing how each reinforces the other. It highlights the importance of altering limiting beliefs to foster more positive thought patterns and vice versa.

Objective: To provide readers with a framework for understanding how changing their beliefs can lead to more empowering thoughts and behaviors.

Overcoming Limiting Beliefs and Building Confidence:

Description: This section offers practical steps for identifying and challenging limiting beliefs. It discusses the process of reframing these beliefs into empowering ones and how this transformation builds self-confidence. The role of resilience and persistence in this journey is also covered.

Objective: To empower readers with actionable strategies for overcoming self-doubt and building lasting confidence.

Conclusion of Step 2:

Description: Reinforces the ongoing nature of overcoming limiting beliefs and building confidence, emphasizing that it is a continuous practice essential for personal growth.

Objective: To motivate readers to keep working on their mindset and prepare for the next phase of their journey.

Next Step Reference:

Description: Introduces the next step, which will guide readers through the process of identifying their purpose, setting meaningful goals, and crafting a vision.

Objective: To transition smoothly into the importance of having a clear direction and purpose in life.

Step 3: Identifying Purpose, Goal Setting, and Vision Crafting

Understanding Purpose:

Description: This section explores the concept of purpose, why it is crucial for personal and professional fulfillment, and how to discover it.

It covers exercises and reflections that help readers align their actions and decisions with their core values and long-term aspirations.

Objective: To help readers uncover their deeper motivations and align their goals with their true purpose.

Crafting a Vision for Your Life:

Description: Discusses the importance of having a clear and compelling vision for the future. This section provides guidance on how to create a vision that inspires and directs long-term efforts, turning abstract dreams into achievable realities.

Objective: To equip readers with the tools to visualize their ideal future and use this vision as a motivational and directional tool.

Setting SMART Goals:

Description: Introduces the SMART framework (Specific, Measurable, Achievable, Relevant, Time-bound) for goal setting. It explains how setting SMART goals can provide a clear, actionable plan that bridges the gap between vision and reality.

Objective: To teach readers how to set effective goals that are both ambitious and attainable, ensuring steady progress toward their vision.

Creating a Roadmap to Success:

Description: Focuses on the importance of having a strategic plan or roadmap that breaks down long-term goals into actionable steps. It discusses how to stay on track, measure progress, and make necessary adjustments along the way.

Objective: To provide readers with a practical approach to achieving their vision by creating and following a detailed plan.

Conclusion of Step 3:

Description: Summarizes the importance of having a clear purpose, vision, and goals in guiding personal and professional growth.

Objective: To reinforce the idea that a well-defined roadmap is essential for achieving what may once have seemed impossible.

Next Step Reference:

Description: Introduces the importance of time management, prioritization, and continuous learning as the next areas of focus.

Objective: To transition into the practical skills necessary for maintaining momentum and focus.

Step 4: Time Management, Prioritization, and Continuous Learning

Effective Time Management: Strategies for Success:

Description: This section covers the importance of managing time effectively to maximize productivity and minimize stress. It includes strategies such as time-blocking, scheduling, and avoiding multitasking, along with practical tools like calendars and to-do lists.

Objective: To help readers develop better time management habits that enable them to make the most of each day and stay focused on their goals.

Prioritization: Focusing on What Matters Most:

Description: Discusses the concept of prioritization and its role in achieving significant goals. It introduces tools like the Eisenhower Matrix and the ABC Method to help readers identify and focus on the most important tasks.

Objective: To teach readers how to prioritize effectively, ensuring that they focus their time and energy on tasks that have the most impact.

Continuous Learning: Staying Ahead in a Changing World:

Description: Emphasizes the importance of lifelong learning for staying relevant, adaptable, and innovative. It covers various ways to engage in continuous learning, including online courses, reading, and networking with professionals in the field.

Objective: To encourage readers to embrace continuous learning as a key component of personal and professional development.

Leveraging Social Capital: Building Connections for Success:

Description: Discusses the value of social capital—networks and relationships—as a critical resource for achieving long-term success. It provides strategies for building and leveraging these connections to gain opportunities and support.

Objective: To teach readers how to build and use their social networks effectively to support their continuous learning and growth.

Conclusion of Step 4:

Description: Summarizes the importance of time management, prioritization, and continuous learning in maintaining focus and achieving goals.

Objective: To reinforce the need for these skills in creating a sustainable path to success.

Next Step Reference:

Description: Introduces networking, mentorship, and support systems as the next essential components of success.

Objective: To set the stage for the importance of relationships and community in achieving extraordinary success.

Step 5: Networking, Mentorship, and Support Systems

The Value of Mentorship:

Description: This section emphasizes the significance of mentorship in personal and professional development. It explores how mentors provide guidance, share wisdom, and offer support based on their own experiences, helping you avoid common pitfalls and accelerate your growth.

Objective: To help readers understand the importance of finding and working with a mentor who can guide them through challenges and help them achieve their goals.

Building a Diverse Network:

Description: Discusses the importance of creating a diverse network of contacts from various backgrounds and industries. It explains how a broad network can provide new perspectives, resources, and opportunities, enhancing both personal and professional growth.

Objective: To encourage readers to actively build and maintain a diverse network that can support them in achieving their objectives.

Leveraging Support Systems:

Description: Focuses on the role of support systems, including family, friends, colleagues, and professional networks, in sustaining progress and well-being. It covers how to cultivate and rely on these relationships during challenging times.

Objective: To teach readers how to build and leverage their support systems to maintain resilience and achieve long-term success.

The Role of Collaboration:

Description: This section highlights the benefits of collaboration, including shared knowledge, resources, and skills. It discusses how working together with others can lead to innovative solutions and greater achievements.

Objective: To encourage readers to engage in collaborative efforts as a means of enhancing their success and expanding their capabilities.

Networking Strategies:

Description: Provides practical strategies for effective networking, such as attending industry events, joining professional organizations, and participating in online communities. It also offers tips for maintaining and strengthening these connections over time.

Objective: To equip readers with the tools and techniques needed to build and sustain a strong professional network.

Giving and Receiving Feedback:

Description: Discusses the importance of constructive feedback for personal and professional growth. It covers how to seek feedback from mentors, peers, and networks, as well as how to provide valuable feedback to others.

Objective: To help readers develop a culture of open communication and continuous improvement through effective feedback.

The Power of Peer Support:

Description: Explores the benefits of peer support groups or communities, which provide mutual encouragement, shared experiences, and collective problem-solving. This section emphasizes the value of belonging to a supportive peer group.

Objective: To encourage readers to seek out and actively participate in peer support networks to enhance their resilience and motivation.

Conclusion of Step 5:

Description: Summarizes the importance of mentorship, networking, and support systems in achieving personal and professional success. It reinforces the idea that building and maintaining strong relationships is crucial for long-term growth.

Objective: To reinforce the critical role that relationships and community play in sustaining progress and achieving success.

Next Step Reference:

Description: Introduces the concept of resilience, learning from failure, and embracing risk as the next essential components of success.

Objective: To prepare readers for the challenges and growth opportunities that come with developing resilience and taking calculated risks.

Step 6: Resilience, Learning from Failure, and Embracing Risk

Building Mental Toughness:

Description: This section covers techniques for developing mental toughness, which is the ability to persevere through challenges, stay focused under pressure, and remain resilient in the face of setbacks. It emphasizes the importance of self-discipline, goal-setting, and maintaining a positive mindset.

Objective: To help readers build the mental strength needed to navigate obstacles and achieve their goals.

Learning from Failure:

Description: Discusses the value of failure as a learning opportunity. This section explores how to analyze failures, extract valuable lessons, and use those insights to improve future efforts. It encourages readers to view setbacks as stepping stones to success.

Objective: To teach readers how to embrace failure as a necessary part of the growth process and use it to fuel their progress.

Embracing Risk:

Description: This section highlights the importance of taking calculated risks for personal and professional growth. It discusses how to assess risks, make informed decisions, and step out of your comfort zone to achieve extraordinary results.

Objective: To encourage readers to take bold actions that align with their goals, understanding that risk-taking is essential for innovation and success.

Strategies for Overcoming Adversity:

Description: Provides practical strategies for overcoming adversity, such as maintaining a positive outlook, seeking support, and staying committed to your goals. This section emphasizes the importance of resilience in navigating difficult situations.

Objective: To help readers develop a resilient mindset that enables them to overcome obstacles and continue striving toward their objectives.

The Growth Mindset in Action:

Description: Explores how adopting a growth mindset can help readers embrace challenges, persist in the face of setbacks, and see effort as the path to mastery. This section highlights the power of a growth mindset in achieving long-term success.

Objective: To encourage readers to cultivate a growth mindset that drives continuous learning and improvement.

Resilience in Practice:

Description: Discusses practical ways to build resilience, such as developing strong relationships, practicing self-care, and maintaining a sense of purpose. This section provides actionable steps for enhancing resilience in daily life.

Objective: To provide readers with practical tools and strategies for building and maintaining resilience.

Conclusion of Step 6:

Description: Summarizes the key elements of resilience, learning from failure, and embracing risk as essential components of personal and professional growth. It reinforces the importance of these qualities in achieving success.

Objective: To highlight the value of resilience, adaptability, and risk-taking in overcoming challenges and reaching your full potential.

Next Step Reference:

Description: Introduces the importance of celebrating milestones, sustaining progress, and giving back to your community as the final step in achieving extraordinary success.

Objective: To prepare readers for the culmination of their journey by focusing on reflection, celebration, and contribution to others.

Step 7: Developing Character, Celebrating Milestones, and Sustaining Progress

Character Development: The Foundation of Lasting Success

Description: This section emphasizes the importance of character traits such as adaptability, humility, integrity, perseverance, self-discipline, and trust in achieving and sustaining long-term success. It highlights that while talents and gifts can open doors, it is character that ensures continued success and growth.

Objective: To encourage readers to focus on cultivating and integrating these character traits into their daily lives as a foundation for ongoing achievement and fulfillment.

Celebrating Milestones: Recognizing Achievements

Description: This part of the chapter discusses the significance of celebrating milestones as a way to acknowledge progress, reinforce positive behaviors, and maintain motivation. It explores how recognizing achievements contributes to sustained progress and encourages further development.

Objective: To motivate readers to regularly celebrate their achievements, using these moments to reflect on their growth and reinforce the character traits that have supported their journey.

Sustaining Progress: Maintaining Momentum Over Time

Description: This section focuses on the importance of continuous growth and adaptability to maintain the momentum gained from previous achievements. It covers strategies such as ongoing learning, personal development, and engaging in meaningful activities that support long-term progress.

Objective: To provide readers with practical strategies for sustaining their progress and ensuring that their journey of growth continues beyond initial milestones.

Giving Back: The Role of Service in Personal Growth

Description: This part highlights the value of giving back to others through teaching, mentoring, and community service. It emphasizes how sharing knowledge, experiences, and resources not only solidifies personal success but also creates a positive impact on the broader community.

Objective: To inspire readers to incorporate service into their lives as a way to enhance their own growth and contribute to the growth of others, creating a ripple effect of empowerment and inspiration.

Avoiding Negative Outlets and Influences

Description: This section discusses the importance of avoiding negative influences that can derail progress. It offers insights into how staying connected to positive environments and communities, such as through volunteering and engagement in supportive networks, can help maintain focus and discipline.

Objective: To guide readers in making conscious choices to avoid negative influences and stay aligned with their goals and values.

Conclusion of Step 7: Embrace Growth and Pay It Forward

Description: The conclusion ties together the key themes of character development, celebrating milestones, sustaining progress, and giving back. It reinforces the idea that these practices are essential for achieving and sustaining extraordinary success.

Objective: To encourage readers to embrace these practices fully, recognizing their extraordinary potential and using it to leave a lasting impact on the world around them.

INDEX

GLOSSARY

ABC Method:
A prioritization technique that categorizes tasks into three groups: A (most important), B (important but not urgent), and C (least important).

Adaptability: The ability to adjust one's thoughts, behaviors, and strategies in response to changing circumstances. It is a key trait for thriving in a rapidly changing world and is deeply connected to resilience.

Affirmations:
Positive statements repeated to oneself with the intention of instilling confidence, reinforcing positive beliefs, or encouraging specific outcomes.

Automatic Negative Thoughts (ANTs):
Repetitive, involuntary negative thoughts that often distort reality and contribute to feelings of anxiety, depression, and low self-esteem.

Behavioral Activation:
A therapeutic approach that encourages individuals to engage in meaningful or enjoyable activities to counteract depression and improve mood.

Beliefs:
Convictions or acceptances that certain things are true or real. They shape our perceptions, decisions, and actions.

Benevolence:

The perception that a trustee has the trustor's best interests at heart, a key component of trust.

Burnout:

A state of emotional, physical, and mental exhaustion caused by prolonged stress, often associated with work or overwhelming responsibilities.

Cognitive-Behavioral Therapy (CBT):

An evidence-based psychological treatment that helps individuals identify and modify dysfunctional beliefs and thought patterns to improve mental health.

Comfort Zone:

A psychological state in which a person feels familiar, safe, and at ease. Operating within this zone can limit growth and learning opportunities.

Competence:

The ability of a person or leader to perform tasks they are entrusted with, contributing to the development of trust.

Continuous Learning:

The ongoing process of acquiring new knowledge and skills throughout one's life to stay relevant and adaptable.

Core Values:

Fundamental beliefs or guiding principles that dictate behavior and action. They help individuals make decisions aligned with their true self.

Culture of Genius:

A mindset or environment that emphasizes innate talent as the key to success. This culture often fosters a fixed mindset, where individuals believe that abilities are static and avoid challenges that might expose their perceived limitations.

Culture of Growth:

A mindset or environment that emphasizes effort, learning, and resilience as the paths to success. In this culture, individuals adopt a growth mindset, believing that abilities can be developed through hard work and dedication, encouraging them to embrace challenges and view failures as opportunities for growth.

Eisenhower Matrix:

A time management tool that helps prioritize tasks by urgency and importance, dividing them into four quadrants: Urgent & Important, Important but Not Urgent, Urgent but Not Important, and Not Urgent & Not Important.

Efficiency:

The ability to accomplish a task with the minimum expenditure of time, effort, or resources. Efficiency is about doing things in the best possible way.

Effectiveness:

The degree to which something is successful in producing a desired result. It's about doing the right things to achieve your goals.

Emotional Intelligence (EI):

The ability to recognize, understand, and manage one's own emotions, as well as the emotions of others. High EI contributes to better relationships, decision-making, and personal well-being.

Empowering Beliefs:

Positive convictions that inspire confidence, motivation, and action, enabling individuals to achieve their goals and improve well-being.

Feedback Loop:

A process where the outcomes of a system or action are fed back into the system to regulate or guide future behavior, often used in personal development to improve performance.

Fixed Mindset:

A belief that abilities and intelligence are static and cannot be changed, often leading to avoidance of challenges and fear of failure.

Flow State:

A mental state in which a person is fully immersed in an activity, characterized by a sense of energized focus, full involvement, and enjoyment in the process.

Forward Thinking:

The practice of planning for the future by anticipating changes, challenges, and opportunities. It involves strategic planning, setting long-term goals, and being proactive in responding to potential scenarios rather than simply reacting to current situations.

Goal Alignment:

The process of ensuring that individual goals are in harmony with one's overall mission, vision, and purpose, creating a cohesive plan for success.

Grit:

A combination of passion and perseverance toward long-term goals. Grit is seen as a key predictor of success.

Groupthink:

A psychological phenomenon where the desire for harmony or conformity in a group results in irrational or dysfunctional decision-making. It often leads to the suppression of dissenting opinions and a lack of critical thinking.

Growth Mindset:

A belief that abilities and intelligence can be developed through effort, learning, and persistence, leading to greater resilience and a willingness to embrace challenges.

Hedonic Treadmill:

The tendency of humans to quickly return to a relatively stable level of happiness despite major positive or negative events or life changes. This concept highlights the importance of finding contentment from within rather than from external achievements.

Humility: The quality of having a modest view of one's own importance, which involves recognizing one's strengths and weaknesses, being open to learning from others, and maintaining a balanced perspective on achievements and limitations.

Impostor Syndrome:

A psychological pattern where an individual doubts their accomplishments and fears being exposed as a fraud, despite evident success.

Integrity: The adherence to moral and ethical principles, involving honesty, trustworthiness, and consistency in actions across all areas of life. It is essential for building trust and sustaining long-term success.

Intrinsic Motivation:

The drive to perform an activity for its inherent satisfaction or personal reward, rather than for some external consequence.

Learned Helplessness:

A condition in which a person suffers from a sense of power-lessness, arising from a traumatic event or persistent failure to succeed. This concept was developed by Martin Seligman, and it explains why some people may give up on goals or challenges due to repeated failures.

Locus of Control:

A concept referring to the degree to which people believe they have control over the outcomes of events in their lives. A person with an internal locus of control believes they can influence events and outcomes.

Mental Toughness:

The ability to persevere through difficulties, stay focused under pressure, and remain resilient in the face of adversity. Mental toughness is often associated with determination, resilience, and the capacity to recover from setbacks.

Mindset:

A set of beliefs or attitudes that shape an individual's perception of themselves, others, and the world. It influences how one approaches challenges and opportunities.

Mindfulness:

The practice of being fully present and engaged in the moment, aware of your thoughts, feelings, and surroundings without judgment.

Mission:

The specific, actionable steps and goals that define what you intend to achieve in life or within a specific endeavor. Your mission outlines what you do and how you do it in alignment with your purpose.

Mission Statement:

A formal summary of the aims and values of an individual or organization. It defines what one intends to achieve and how they plan to accomplish it.

MoSCoW Method:

A prioritization technique that categorizes tasks into Must have, Should have, Could have, and Won't have, based on their importance.

Move Fast and Break Things:

A concept popularized by Facebook that encourages rapid innovation and experimentation, even at the risk of making mistakes. While it promotes agility and speed, it is essential to balance this approach with the need for quality and effectiveness.

Negative Thoughts:

Destructive and pessimistic thoughts that focus on potential failures, negatives in situations, and self-doubt, often leading to anxiety and depression.

Neuroplasticity:

The brain's ability to reorganize itself by forming new neural connections throughout life. This ability is crucial for learning and adapting to new experiences.

Networking:

The process of building and maintaining relationships with others, often for professional or personal gain, providing mutual support and opportunities.

Oxytocin:

A hormone associated with social bonding and trust, sometimes referred to as the "love hormone."

Patience: The ability to endure delays, difficulties, or adversity without becoming frustrated or discouraged. It complements perseverance by ensuring that actions are well-timed and sustainable over the long term.

Perseverance: The sustained effort and determination to achieve long-term goals despite challenges, setbacks, or failures. It is closely related to patience and is a key driver of personal and professional success.

Positive Psychology:

A branch of psychology that focuses on the study of positive aspects of the human experience, such as happiness, well-being, and flourishing.

Positive Realistic Thoughts:

Optimistic thoughts that are grounded in reality. They acknowledge challenges and obstacles but maintain a constructive outlook focused on actionable solutions.

Predictability:

The consistent behavior of an individual that reinforces trust over time.

Procrastination:

The act of delaying or postponing tasks or decisions, often leading to stress and decreased productivity.

Psychological Reactance:

A motivational reaction to offers, persons, rules, or regulations that threaten or eliminate specific behavioral freedoms. When people feel their freedom to choose is restricted, they often react by asserting their independence, which can lead to resistance to change.

Purpose:

The underlying reason for one's actions and decisions. It provides direction and motivation, contributing to a sense of fulfillment and resilience.

Resilience:

The ability to recover quickly from difficulties, adapt to change, and continue moving forward despite challenges or setbacks.

Resilience Building:

The process of developing the mental and emotional fortitude to recover from adversity, adapt to change, and keep going in the face of challenges.

Self-Awareness:

The conscious knowledge of one's own character, feelings, motives, and desires. Self-awareness is essential for personal growth and effective decision-making.

Self-Confidence:

A belief in one's abilities to achieve goals and navigate life's challenges effectively. It can be cultivated through intentional practices and positive self-reinforcement.

Self-Discipline: The ability to control one's impulses, emotions, and behaviors to stay focused on long-term goals. It involves resisting short-term gratifications and is critical for maintaining consistent progress toward achieving success.

Self-Efficacy:

The belief in one's ability to succeed in specific situations or accomplish a task. High self-efficacy can lead to greater motivation and perseverance.

SMART Goals:

A goal-setting framework that stands for Specific, Measurable, Achievable, Relevant, and Time-bound, helping to create clear and actionable goals.

Social Capital:

The networks and relationships that provide support, resources, and opportunities, contributing to personal and professional success.

Stress Management:

The techniques and strategies used to control and reduce stress levels, ensuring that stress does not negatively impact one's physical and mental health.

SWOT Analysis:

A strategic planning tool used to identify Strengths, Weaknesses, Opportunities, and Threats. It is often used in personal and professional development to assess potential strategies.

Time Blocking:

A time management technique where specific time slots are allocated for different tasks or activities, helping to ensure focus and productivity.

Trust:

The reliance on or confidence in the dependability of someone or something. In interpersonal relationships, trust represents the confidence that one person or group has in another's reliability and predictability.

Vision:

A clear, aspirational picture of what success looks like in the future. It represents the ultimate goal or destination you aim to achieve, guiding your actions and decisions along the way.

Vision Statement:

A forward-looking declaration of an individual's or organization's aspirations and desired future. It serves as a guide for setting goals and making decisions.

Visualization:

The practice of creating detailed mental images of a desired outcome or goal as a way to enhance motivation and focus on achieving that goal.

Warmth:

A component of trust based on kindness, empathy, and genuine care for others, often prioritized over competence in trust formation.

Work-Life Balance:

The equilibrium between personal life and professional responsibilities. Achieving work-life balance is key to maintaining overall well-being and avoiding burnout.

ABOUT THE AUTHOR

Desmond Eric Ketter is a dedicated behavioral health practitioner with years of personal and professional experience in mental health. He is devoted to guiding children, teenagers, and young adults through the complexities of mental and emotional wellness as a licensed professional counselor. He earned a Bachelor of Science degree in Psychology, with a minor in Social Welfare, from Northeastern State University, and holds a Master's degree in Clinical Mental Health Counseling from the University of Oklahoma. Beyond his professional life, Desmond is married to Pheona, and together they have five incredible children. Additionally, he is the vice president of the Liberian Community Association of Tulsa and serves as an elder and youth coordinator at his local church, where he has been a committed member for over a decade.

You can connect with Desmond on:

Website: https://desmondketter.com

Twitter: https://twitter.com/desmondericketter

Facebook: https://www.facebook.com/desmond.ketter.9

Instagram: https://www.instagram.com/desmondketter

TikTok: https://www.tiktok.com/@counselordesmond

For Questions or Comments:

Contact: https://desmondketter.com/pages/contact

Stay Connected

Scan the QR code to leave a review, follow updates, discover new books, and find out about upcoming events and specials. Your engagement means the world and thank you for being part of this community!

ALSO AVAILABLE FROM

Desmond Eric Ketter

The Unbreakable Human Spirit of Resilience: A Boy's Journey from Adversity to Triumph tells the inspiring story of Ericboy, a young boy who overcomes the hardships of war-torn Liberia and the challenges of adapting to life in the United States. From the slums of West Point to his eventual success as a mental health counselor, Ericboy's journey is a testament to resilience, determination, and the power of the human spirit to turn adversity into opportunity.

Legacy Lantern Publishing House

www.desmondketter.com

www.ingramcontent.com/pod-product-compliance
Lightning Source LLC
Chambersburg PA
CBHW030408130626
46549CB00004B/1680